READWELL'S

LEAR
IN A MONTH

Easy Method of Learning Arabic
Through English Without a Teacher

Mrs. Rekha Chawla
B.A. (Cairo)

Readwell Publications
NEW DELHI-110008

Published by :
READWELL PUBLICATIONS
B-8, Rattan Jyoti, 18, Rajendra Place
New Delhi-110 008 (INDIA)
Phone : 5737448, 5712649, 5721761
Fax : 91-11-5812385
E-mail : readwell@sify.com
newlight@vsnl.net

ISBN 81-87782-13-7

Printed at : Arya Offset Press, New Delhi.

PREFACE

At a time when there is a great rush of Indians to the Arab countries in view of better employment opportunities there, it has become essential to have a working knowledge of the Arabic language for those who are going there. This facilitates their living among the Arabs and makes their day-to-day life easy.

In view of this need, we have pleasure in bringing out a book on the teaching of the Arabic language through the media of English and Hindi. We have divided the whole book into many parts and have given a few lessons on basic grammar. The difficulty with the Arabic language is that it is spoken and written differently in different Arab countries. Sometimes the difference is so great that a person from one Arab country cannot understand the Arabic spoken in another Arab country. We have, therefore, tried to teach in such a way that the learner will feel at home in any Arab country even though he may not be completely conversant with the language of the area in which he is living. We have added a few pages of vocabulary also to facilitate a working knowledge of the essential parts of the language. We have every hope that the learners will be happy with this small work. We shall always be happy to receive any constructive suggestions for improving this work still further.

Authors

CONTENTS

—

Lesson 1

The Arabic Alphabet
अरबी अक्षर माला

English	Hindi	Arabic	Pronunciation
a	अ	अलिफ़	alef
b	ब	बा	ba
t	त	ता	ta
th	त्	ता	tha
j	ज	जीम्	jeem
h	ह्	हा	ha
kh	ख्	खे	kha
d	द	दान्	dal
th	द्	दाल्	thal
r	र	रा	ra
z	ज़	ज़ा	zien
c,s	स	सीन्	seen
sh	श	शीन्	sheen
ss	स्	सुवाद	ssad
dh	व.	दुवाद	ded
t	त.	त.ा	tah
z	ज.	ज.ा	zah
ei	अ	अे न्	ein

(7)

gh	ग्रैन्	ग़ैन्	gheim
q	क़ाफ़्	क़ाफ़्	quaf
k	क	काफ़्	kaf
f	फ़	फ़े	fa
l	ल	लाम्	lam
m	म	मीम्	meem
n	न	नुन्	noon
h	ह	हे	ha
w	ब	वाब्	wa
y	य	या	ya

▬▬

Lesson 2

Parts of Speech
शब्दभेद

There are eight parts of speech :

English	Hindi	Arabic	Arabic pronunciation
Noun	संज्ञा	Issm	ईसम
Pronoun	सर्वनाम	Dhamir	जमीर
Adjective	विशेषण	sifat	सिफ़त
Verb	क्रिया	fiel	फंयल
Adverb	क्रिया विशेषण	zarf	जर्फ़
Preposition	सम्बन्ध बोधक अव्यय	harfejarr	हर्फेजार
Conjunction	समुच्चयबोधक	harfeataf	हर्फे अतफ
Interjection	विस्मयबोधक	harfe nidaa	हर्फेनिदा

NOUN : Noun is that part of speech by which we understand the name of person, thing or place. (संज्ञा वह शब्द है जिसके द्वारा किसी व्यक्ति, जीव, वस्तु अथवा स्थान आदि का पता लगता है) ।

EXAMPLE

English	Hindi	Arabic	Pronunciation
dog	कुत्ता	kalb	कल्लब
horse	धोड़ा	hisan	हिसान

(9)

cat	बिल्ली	kitta	कित्ता
man	आदमी	rajul	राजुल
street	सड़क	sharah	शारिह

PRONOUN : The pronoun is a word which takes the place of a noun (सर्वनाम वह शब्द है जो संज्ञा के स्थान पर आता है)

EXAMPLE

English	Hindi	Arabic	Pronunciation
I	मैं	ana	अना
you	तुम	enta, enti	इन्ता, इन्ती
he	वह	hu b	हु ब
she	वह	he ya	हि य
it	यह	hu-b, he-ya	हु ब हि य
we	हम	nehnu	नहनु
you (plural)	तुम लोग	antum,	अन्तुम
		antun-na	अन्तुन-न
they	वे	hum	हुम

ADJECTIVE : Adjective is a word which tells about the quality of a noun or pronoun (संज्ञा अथवा सर्वनाम की विशेषता बताने वाले शब्द की विशेषण कहते हैं)

EXAMPLE

English	Hindi	Arabic	Pronunciation
big	बड़ा	kaber	काबीर
long	लम्बा	towli	तोली
thick	मोटा	katif	कतीफ
fast	तेज़	saria	सरिया
hard	कठिन	sab	साब

VERB : A verb is a word which denotes the action of the subject (क्रिया उसे कहते हैं जिसके द्वारा किसी कार्य के करने अथवा होने का ज्ञान हो) ।

EXAMPLE

English	Hindi	Arabic	Pronunciation
to pay	देना	dafa-yedfa	दफा-यिदफा
to wash	धोना	gasala	गसला
to remember	याद रखना	dakara	दकरा
to call	बुलाना	saha	साहा
to kill	कतल करना	qatal-yaqtul	कतल-यिक्तुल
to accept	मानना	yaqbul	यकबूल
to abandon	छोड़ देना	yatruk	यत्रूक
to reach or arrive	पहुँचना	yasil	यसिल
to invite	दावत देना	yad-oo	यद्ऊ
to revolt	बगावत करना	yasoor	यसूर

ADVERB : An adverb is a word wkich tells the quality or characteristics of a verb.

(क्रिया विशेषण वह है जिसके द्वारा क्रिया की किसी विशेषता का बोध होता है)

EXAMPLE

English	Hindi	Arabic	Pronunciation
slow	धीमा	bati	बाती
high	ऊंचा	ala	अला
low	नीचा	sufl	सुफल
quickly	जल्दी से	bi-suria	बिसुरम्:

PREPOSITION : A preposition is a word which is placed before a noun or pronoun to show its relation with something else.

(सम्बन्धबोधक अव्यय वे शब्द हैं जो संज्ञा या सर्वनाम के वाक्य के साथ सम्बन्ध का ज्ञान कराते हैं)

EXAMPLE

English	Hindi	Arabic	Pronunciation
again	दुबारा	thani atan	थानी आटन
above	ऊपर	faoque	फै औक्यो
below	नीचे	taht, asfal	टहट, असफल
upon	पर	ala	अला
near	पास	qorb	कोर्ब
over	ऊपर	faoque	फै औक्यो
in	में	fi	फी
with	साथ	ma	मए
of	का	min	मिन
without	बिना	bidoon	बिदून
who	जोकि, कौन	alti min	अल्लती मिन

CONJUNCTION : A word used to join one sentence, one word with another sentence or word (जो शब्द एक वाक्य अथवा शब्द को दूसरे वाक्य अथवा शब्द के साथ जोड़ता है उसे समुच्चय-बोधक कहते हैं)

EXAMPLE

English	Hindi	Arabic	Pronunciation
and	और	thomma, wa	थोमा-वा
also	भी	aidan	एदन
but	लेकिन, परन्तु	wala ken	वालाकेन

| which | कौन सा | enhu | इन्हु |
| both | दोनों | keela | किला |

INTERJECTION : An interjection is a word which expresses some sudden feeling of the mind (विस्मयबोधक वह शब्द है जिसके द्वारा मन की किसी भावना की एकदम बोध होता है)

EXAMPLE

English	Hindi	Arabic	Pronunciation
oh	ओह	yaa	या
O my lord	हे परमात्मा	yaa rabee	यारबी

Lesson 3

Number
वचन

There are two numbers——singular (mafarad) and plural (Jamah)

In Arabic the plural is formed by adding wau, wa, noon (ayn) to the singular.

EXAMPLE

Singular	Plural
a pen (kalam) एक कलम	two pens (kalamayn) दो कलमें

We give below a brief list of some numbers :

	Eng.	Hindi	Arabic	Pronunciation
Sing.	boy	लड़का	waladu	वलदु
Plu.	boys	लड़के	aulad	औलाद
Sing.	child	बच्चा	tifal	तिफ़ल
Plu.	children	बच्चे	atfal	अतफ़ाल
Sing.	girl	लड़की	bint	बिन्त
Plu.	girls	लड़कियां	banat	बनात
Sing.	donkey	गधा	himar	हिमार
Plu.	donkeys	गधे	hamir	हमीर
Sing.	knife	चाकू	sakak	सकाक
Plu.	knives	बहुत चाकू	sakakin	सकाकीन
Sing.	thief	चोर	lass	लस्स

(14)

Plu.	thieves	बहुत चोर	lusus	लुसुस
Sing.	man	आदमी	rajul	रजुल
Plu.	men	बहुत आदमी	rijaal	रिजाल
Sing.	woman	औरत	em-ra atun	इम् रा अतुन
Plu.	women	औरतें	nisa	निसा
Sing.	foot	पैर	kadam	कदम
Plu.	feet	बहुत पैर	akdaam	अक़्दाम
Sing.	tooth	दांत	sin	सिन
Plu.	teeth	बहुत दांत	asnan	अस्नान
Sing.	city	शहर	Madina	मदीना
Plu.	cities	बहुत शहर	mudun	मुदुन
Sing.	family	परिवार	aeela	आइला
Plu.	families	कई परिवार	aeeslat	आइलात
Sing.	maid servant	नौकरानी	khadeema	खादीमा
Plu.	maid servants	नौकरानियां	khadeema- tayan	खादीमातायन
Sing.	wife	पत्नी	zoaja	जौजा
Plu.	wives	पत्नियां	zoajat	जोजात
Sing.	writer	लेखक	katib	कातिब
Plu.	writers	कई लेखक	katibun	कातिबून
Sing.	hat	हैट (टोपी)	barnita	बर्नीता
Plu.	hats	कई हैट	baraneet	बरानीत
Sing.	day	दिन	yaom	यौम
Plu.	days	कई दिन	ayaam	अयाम
Sing.	dress	कपड़ा	fistaan	फ़िस्तान
Plu.	dresses	कई कपड़े	fasateen	फ़सातीन
Sing.	monkey	बंदर	kirad	क़िरद

Plu.	monkeys	कई बंदर	kiradtun or kurud	क़िरदतुन or कुरुद
Sing.	key	चाबी	miftaah	मिफ़्ताह
Plu.	keys	चाबियां	mafateeh	मफ़ातीह
Sing.	watch	घड़ी	saa'a	सा'आह
Plu.	watches	घड़ियां	saa'aat	साआत
Sing.	nurse	सेविका	mumarrida	मुमारिदा
Plu.	nurses	सेविकाएं	mumarridat	मुमारीदात
Sing.	a thing	वस्तु	haaja	हाजा
Plu.	things	वस्तुएं	haajaat	हाजात
Sing.	house	घर	bayt	बयत
Plu.	houses	कई घर	buyoot	बुयुत
Sing.	partner	साथी	shareek	शारीक
Plu.	partners	कई साथी	shurakaa	शुरग्रका
Sing.	language	भाषा	lessan	लिसान
Plu.	languages	भाषाएँ	alsenah	अलसिना
Sing.	poor	गरीब	faqeer	फकीर
Plu.	poor (many)	कई गरीब	fuqaraa	फुकारा
Sing.	office	दफ्तर	maktak	मकतक
Plu.	offices	कई दफ्तर	makaateb	मकातिब
Sing.	handker-chief	रूमाल	mandeel	मनदील
Plu.	handker-chiefs	कई रूमाल	manaadeel	मनादील
Sing.	heart	दिल	qalab	कलब
Plu.	hearts	कई दिल	quloob	कुलूब
Sing.	camel	ऊंट	jamal	जमाल

Plu.	camels	कई ऊंट	jemaal	जिमाल
Sing.	book	पुस्तक	ketaab	किताब
Plu.	books	पुस्तकें	kutub	कुतुब
Sing.	bag	थैला	haqiiba	हकीबा
Plu.	bags	थैले	haqaa-ib	हकाइब
Sing.	river	नदी	nahr	नाहर
Plu.	rivers	नदियां	anhur	अनहुर
Sing.	month	मास	shahr	शाहर
Plu.	months	कई मास	ashhur	अशाहुर
Sing.	market	मंडी	sooq	सूक
Plu.	markets	मंडियां	aswaaq	असवाक
Sing.	door	दरवाज़ा	al-bab	अल-बाब
Plu.	doors	दरवाज़े	alabol	अल-अबोल

USE IN SENTENCES

Sing.	The teacher came अध्यापक आया	atal mualim अतल मुअल्लिम
Plu.	The teachers came अध्यापक आए	atal mualimeen अतल मुअल्लिमीन
Sing.	I saw the teacher मैंने अध्यापक को देखा	ana shift el moualem अना शिफ़्तुल मुअल्लिम
Plu.	I saw the teachers मैंने अध्यापक देखे	ana shift el moulameen अना शिफ़्तुल मुअल्लिमीन
Sing.	The boy is sitting लड़का बैठा हुआ है	al waldu jalis sun अल् वलदु जालि सुन
Plu.	The boys are sitting लड़के बैठे हुए हैं	al awaladu jaalisun अल् औलादु जालिसून
Sing.	The girl is sitting लड़की बैठी हुई है	al bintu jaalis tun अल् बिनतु जालितून

Plu.	The girls are sitting	al banatu jaa lisa tun
	लड़कियाँ बैठी हुई हैं	अल् बनातु जालिसातुन्
Sing.	This is a car	ha da hi sayartun
	यह एक कार है	हा दा हि संयारतुन्
Plu.	These are cars	ha da hi sayaratun
	यह कारें हैं	हा दा हि संयारातुन्

From the above examples, it is clear Arabic plurals are formed in many ways.

(ऊपर दिये गए उदाहरणों से पता चलता है कि अरबी भाषा में बहुवचन कई प्रकार से बनते हैं)

EXAMPLE

1. With masculine the word gets a suffix "yeen" as in (पुलिंग शब्दों के अन्त में "यीन" जोड़ा जाता है) जैसे— muallemun (teacher) अध्यापक—muallemeen (teachers) कई अध्यापक

2. With feminine the word gets a suffix "aat" as in (स्त्रीलिंग शब्दों के अन्त में "आत" लगाया जाता है, जैसे mumarrida (nurse) नर्स—mumarridaat (nurses) नर्सें

3. There are Arabic words which form their plurals with the help of endings in "aam", "aad", as in

(कुछ अरबी शब्दों का बहुवचन रूप "आम", "आद", के द्वारा बनता है, जैसे)

kalam (pen) कलम	aklaam (pens) कलमें
walad (boy) लड़का	awlaad (boys) लड़के

4. In some words plurals are formed with the help of suffixes as well as prefixes, example :

(कुछ शब्दों में बहुवचन बनाने के लिए शब्द के प्रारम्भ तथा बाद में कुछ अक्षर जोड़े जाते हैं, जैसे:

lebaas (dress) कपड़ा   albesah (dresses) कपड़े

lesaan (language) भाषा   alsenah (languages) भाषाएँ

5. In some other cases the 'aa' sound is added within the singular word to make it plural, as in

(कुछ अन्य एक वचन शब्दों में 'aa' बीच में जोड़ने से उनका बहुवचन बनाया जाता है, जैसे—

manzel (house) घर   manaazel (houses) कई घर

From the above we know the several ways of forming plural in the Arabic language. For a beginner, it is confusing but after some practice difficulty remains no more.

(ऊपर दिए गए उदाहरणों से बहुवचन बनाने के कई उपायों का बोध होता है । आरम्भ में यह सब कुछ कठिन जान पड़ता है परन्तु अभ्यास से भी कठिनाइयाँ दूर हो जाती हैं)

Some other Singulars & Plurals

	English	Hindi	Arabic	Pronun.
Sing.	This (mas)	यह	hatha (mas)	हादा
			lilkareeb (fem)	लिलक़रीब
Plu.	These	ये	haola	हाओला
Sing.	That (mas)	वह	thaka (mas)	थाका
			lilbaed (fem)	लिलब्यीद:
Plu.	Those	वे	olaik	ओलेवक

Lesson 4

Gender

लिंग

There are **two** genders—masculine and feminine

लिंग दो होते हैं—स्त्रीलिंग, पुल्लिंग

Masculine		*Feminine*	
boy	sabi	girl	bint
लड़का	साबी	लड़की	बिन्त
man	rajol	woman	sayida
आदमी	रजोल	स्त्री	सैयिदा
baby	radhih	baby	radiha
बच्चा	राधिह	बच्ची	राधीहा
child	ti'l	child	tiffla
बच्चा	तिफ़्ल	बच्ची	तिफ़्ला
infant	yafih	infant	yafih
बच्चा	याफ़िह	बच्ची	याफ़िह
lad	gholam, fata	lass	fatat
लड़का	गोलाम, फाता	लड़की	फ़ातात
youth	shab	young lady	shabba
नवयुवक	शाब	नवयुवती	शाबा
bachelor	aanis	single woman	azba
कंवारा	आनिस	कंवारी	अज़बा
bridegroom	arees	bride	arous
दुलहा	अरीस	दुल्हन	अरुस

(20)

married man	motazawij	married woman	motazawija
विवाहित	मोतज़ाविज	विवाहिता	मोताज़ाविजा
divorced man	motallaqu	divorced woman	mautallaqua
तलाक वाला पुरुष	मोतालाकु	तलाक़वाली स्त्री	मोतालाकुआ
father	ab	mother	omm
पिता	अब	माँ	ओम्म
brother	akh	sister	okht
भाई	अख	बहन	अखत
uncle	am, khal	aunt	amma, khala
चाचा	अम, खाल	चाची	अम्मा, खाला
son	walad or iben	daughter	bint
बेटा	वालद या इबीन	बेटी	बिन्त
husband	zouj, rayel	wife	zoujeh, mara
पति	ज़ावज, रायील	पत्नी	ज़ावज़ोह, मारा
nephew	iben or walad-o-ah-khow	niece	bint or o ah-khow
भतीजा	इबीन या खो वालद-ओ-आह	भतीजी	बिन्त—ओ-आह-खो
	iben or walad ekhet	niece	bint ekheet
भांजा	इबीन या वालद ekhet	भांजी	बिन्त ईखीत

grandfather	jidd	grandmother	jiddah
दादा, नाना	जिदद	दादी, नानी	जिददाह
grandson	hafeed	granddaughter	hafeedah
पोता, दोहता	हाफीद	पोती, दोहती	हाफीदाह
stepfather	zouge-el·om	stepmother	zougat-el-ab
सौतेला बाप	ज़ोग इल उम	सौतेली माता	ज़ोगत-इल-अब
god father	ishbeen	god mother	ishbeena
धर्मपिता	इशबीन	धर्ममाता	इशबीना
son-in-law	sihar	daughter-in-law	kinna
जमाता	सिहर	वहु	किन्ना
mr.	saiyid	mrs.	sit
श्रीमान	सैयिद	श्रीमति	सित
male	dakar	female	untha
पुरुष	दाकार	स्त्री	उंथा
he	howa	she	heya
वह	होवा	वह स्त्री	हीया
donkey	himar	ass	himara
गधा	हिमार	गधी	हिमारा
horse	hisan	mare	farass
घोड़ा	हिसान	घोड़ी	फ़रस
ox	thaur	cow	baqara
बैल	सौर	गाय	बक़र:
bull	,,	buffalo	jamoos
भैंसा	,,	भैंस	जामूस
ram	kabsh	sheep	ghanam
मेंढा	कब्श	भेड़	ग़नम
pig	khinzire	sou	khinzira
सूग्रर	खिज़ीर	सूरनी	खिज़ीर:

dog	kalb	bitch	kalba
कुत्ता	कलब	कुतिया	कलब:
tiger	name	tigress	namera
शेर	नमिर	शेरनीं	नमिर:
cock	deek	hen	dajaja
मुर्गा	डीक	मुर्गी	दजाजा
drake	deek but	duck	butta
बतखा	दीक बत	बतख	बत:
peacock	tawoos	peaheu	tawoosa
मोर	ताऊस	मोरनीं	ताऊस:
king	malik	queen	mallika
राजा	मालिक	रानी	मलिका
gentleman	khawaja	lady	sitt
शरीफ पुरुष	खवाजा	शरीफ स्त्री	सित्त

Lesson 5

Verb & Tense
क्रिया तथा काल

There are three tenses in Arabic—present, past and future. (अरबी में तीन काल हैं—वर्तमान, भूत, भविष्यत्)

In Arabic, the sentence begins with the verb as : अरबी भाषा में वाक्य क्रिया से आरम्भ होता है । जैसे :

Past tense (भूत काल) :

boy went	(लड़का गया)
dah bal waladu	(दह बल् वलदु)
boys went	(लड़के गए)
dah bal awladu	(दह बल् औलादु)

In these sentencs the root verb is made of three letters d h b which means "he went." From these we can derive many verbs by conjugating other letters either in the begining or in the middle or at the end.

ऊपर लिखे दो वाक्यों में मूल क्रिया के तीन अक्षर हैं—द ह ब— जिस का अर्थ है "वह गया" । इन तीनों से हम कई अन्य क्रियाएँ बना सकते है यदि इन के शुरु में, बीच में, अथवा अन्त में अन्य अक्षर जोड़ दें ।

See other examples (अन्य उदाहरण) :

She went	(वह गई)
d a h bat	(दह बत्)

they went	(वे गईं)		
da hab n	(द हब् न)		
I went	(मैं गया, गई)		
da hab tu	(द हब् तु)		
we went	(हम गये, गई)		
da hab na	(द हब् ना)		
you went	(तू गया)		
da hab ta	(द हब् त)		
you went	(तुम गए)		
da hab tum	(द हब् तुम)		
he wrote	(उसने लिखा) ka ta b (कतब)		
I went	(मैं गया, मैं गई) da hab tu		
	(द हब् तु)		
	or ana da hab tu		
	(अना द हब् तु)		

The verb can follow the subject also as:

क्रिया कर्ता के बाद में भी आती है जैसे :

boys went	(लड़के गए)	al auladu da ha bu
		(अल् औलादु दहबू)
girls went	(लड़कियाँ गई)	al banatu da ha
		ban
compare	—girls went	da ha ba til banatu

Simple past tense (साधारण भूत काल)

He was	(वह था)	ka-n	(का. न)
they were	(वे थे)	ka-nu	(का नू)
she was	(वह थी)	ka-ntat	(का नूत)
they were	(वे थीं) fem	kunan	(कुन् न)

you were	(तुम थे) sing.	kun-ta	(कुन् त)
" "	plu.	kun-tum	(कुन् तुम)
	fem. sing	kun-ti	(कुन्,ति)
" " fem pl		kun-tun na	(कुन्-तुन् न)
I was	(मैं था)	kun-tu	(कुन्;तु)
we were	(हम थे)	kun-na	(कुन् ना)

Present tense (वर्तमान काल) : In the Arabic language the present is formed from the past tense. The method is to prefix some letters to the verb, as :

अरबी भाषा में वर्तमान काल भूत काल से बनाया जाता है । इसमें क्रिया के शुरु में कुछ अक्षर जोड़े जाते हैं, जैसे :

Past

| played | (खेला) | laiba | (लाई-ब) |

Present

I play	(मैं खेलता हूँ)	Alab	(अल-अब)
he stands	(वह खड़ा होता है)	yoqaf	(योकाफ़)
you stand	(तुम खड़े होते हो)	tuqafum	(तुकाफ़ुम)
you throw	(तू फेंकती है)	tarmin	(तार्मिन)
he goes	(वह जाता है)	ya dah bu	(यदह्,बु)
they go	(वे जाते हैं)	ya da ha bun	(यदहबऊन)
I go	(मैं जाता हूँ)	a dah ab	(अदहब)
he beats	(वह मारता है)	ya daribu	(यद्रिबु)
he writes	(वह लिखता है)	yak tubu	(यक्तुबु)
he breaks	(वह तोड़ता है)	yak siru	(यक्सिरू)

BEGINNING TO WRITE SENTENCES
(वाक्य बनाना आरंभ करें) :

| I am | (मैं हूँ) | Ah-ne-ah or ana | (आह-नी-आह) |

you are	(तुम हो) sing mas	anta	(अन-त)
" "	fem	intay	(इन-ते)
" "	plural	intaw	(इन-ता)
he is	(वह है)	howa	(हु-व)
she is	"	hiye	(हि-य)
it is	(यह है)	hiya au howa	(हि-य-प्रौ हु-व)
we are	(हम हैं)	Ehene-ah	(एहे ने आह)
		or	
		n ahnou	(नहनु)
they are	(वे हैं)	hum hun na	(हुम-हुन न)
I have	(मेरे पास है)	ah-indi	(आह-इन्दी)
we have	(हमारे पास है)	ah-endene-eh	(प्राह-इन्दीनां- एह)
		or	
		indana	(इन्दाना)
you have	(तुम रखते हो)	ah-inda-k	(आह-इन्द-क)
	mas. sing.	or	
		indak	(इन्द-क)
" "	fem sing.	ah-inda-kh	(आह दन्द-खा)
		or	
		inda-kh	
" "	plu	ah-inda-kum	(आह-इन्द- कुम)
		or	
		ind-kum	
he has	(वह रखता है)	ah-ind-hu	(आह-इन्दहू)
		or	
		ind-hu	
he has	(वह रखती है)	ah-indehe-ah	(आ इन्दीही- आह)
		or	
		ind-ha	

they have	(वे रखते है)	ah-indehom or indahom	(आह·इन्दी- होम)

Expressing Possession (स्वामित्व प्रदर्शन करना)

My	(मेरी)	Ee	(ई)
My book	(मेरी पुस्तक)	kitabi	(किताबी)
our	(हमारा, हमारी)	na	ना
our book	(हमारी पुस्तक)	kitabuna	(कितानुना)
our pens	(हमारी कलमें)	aklamuna	(अक्लामुना)
your	(तुम्हारा)	kum	(कुम)
your book	(तुम्हारी पुस्तक)		
	mas.	kitabkum	(किताबकुम)
,, ,,	fem	kitabu-kun-n	(किताबु कुन् न)
,, ,,	(तेरी पुस्तक) fem.	kitabu-ki	(किताबु-कि)
his	(उसका, की)	ho	(हो); ha (हा)
his book	(उसकी पुस्तक)	kitaboho	(किताबुहु)
her book	(,, ,,)	kitaboha	(किताबुहा)
their book	(उनकी पुस्तक)		
	mas.	kitabohom	(किताबु हुम)
,, ,,	fem	kitabohunan	(किताबु हुन् न)
its head	(इसका सर)	rasoha	(रासुहा)

Some other expressions (कुछ अन्य वाक्य)

his copy	(उनकी कापी)	kurrastuha	(कुर्रासतुहा)
their book	(उनकी पुस्तकें)	kutubham	(कुतुबुह् म);
their cars	(इनकी कारें)	sayyaratohom	(सय्यारा- तुहुम);

their copies	(उनकी कापियाँ)	kurrasatuhunan	(कुर्रासातु-
			हुन्न),
your money	(तुम्हारे पैसे)	haka-ibu-kum	(हकाइबुकुम);
your pen	(तुम्हारा कलम)		
	fem.	कलमुकि	(kalamuki)
your hats	(तुम्हारे हैट)	baraneetkom	(वरानीतुकुम)
my car	(मेरी कार)	sayyarati	(सय्याराती)
my key	(मेरी चाबी)	muftaahee	(मुफ्ताही)
our mother	(हमारी माता)	ummenaa	(उम्मीना)
our house	(हमारा घर)	baytenaa	(बायतीना)
my father	(मेरा पिता)	abooya	(अबूया)
our father	(हमारे पिता)	aboona	(अबूना)
your father	(तुम्हारे पिता) sing	abook	(अबूक)
your father	(,,) fem.	abooki	(अबूकी)
your father	(,,) plu.	abookum	(अबूकुम)
your sister	(तुम्हारी बहन)	ukhtik	(उखतिक)
your teacher	(तुम्हारे अध्यापक)	mudarresik	(मुदरिसिक)
your dog	(तुम्हारा कुत्ता)	kalbkum	(कलबकुम)
his father	(उसके पिता)		
	mas.	abooh	(अबू)
her father	(उसके ,,) fem	abooha	(अबूहा)
their father	(उनहे पिता)		
	mas & fem	aboohum	(अबूहुम)
their brother	(उनके भाई) ,,	akhoohum	(अखुहुम)
his hand	(उसका हाथ)	yadoo	(यदू)
boy's book	(लड़के की पुस्तक)	kitab-wl-waldi	(किताब बुल
			बल्दि)

your copies   (अपनी कापियाँ)   kurrasatikum   (कुर्रासतिकुम्)
plu

Next step in sentence forming
(वाक्य-निर्माण का अगला कदम)

this is a book   (यह एक पुस्तक है)
ha da kitabun   (हा दा किताबुन)

this book is mine   (यह मेरी पुस्तक है)
al kitabu li   (अल किताबु ली)

this is a pen   (यह एक कलम है)
ha da kalmun   (हा दा कलमुन)

the pens are ours   (कलम हमारे हैं)
al aklamu lana   (अल अक्लामु लना)

this is a chair   (यह एक कुर्सी है)
ha da kursiyun   (हा दा कुर्सीयुन)

this is an elephant   (यह एक हाथी है)
ha da feelun   (हा दा फीलुन)

the hats are yours   (टोपियां तुम्हारी हैं)
albaranit lakom   (अल-वरानीतु लकुम)

this is a woman   (यह एक स्त्री है)
ha da hi imratun   (हा दा हि इम्र अतुन्)

these are men   (ये पुरुष हैं)
ha ulai rijalun   (हा उलाइ रिजालुन्)

these are women   (ये स्त्रियाँ हैं)
ha ulai nisaon   (हा उलाइ निसाउन्)

those are copies   (बे कापियाँ हैं)
tilak kurrasatun   (तिल्क कुर्रासातुन्)

the food is his   (खाना उसका है)
attaham laha au laho   (अत-तआमु लहा औ लहू)

Forming interrogatives
(प्रश्नसूचक वाक्य बनाने)

In the Arabic language, the addition of 'hal' in the beginning of the sentence turns it into an interrogative.

(अरबी भाषा में वाक्य को प्रश्नसूचक में बदलने के लिए शुरू में "हल्" लगाया जाता है ।

EXAMPLE

you are a student	तुम एक विद्यार्थी हो
ant talibun	अन् तालिबुन्
are you a student ?	क्या तुम विद्यार्थी हो ?
hal ant talibun ?	हल् अनूत तालिबुन ?
you are a driver	तुम चालक हो
ant sayikun	अनत् साईकुन्
are you a driver ?	क्या तुम चालक हो ?
hal ant sayikun ?	हल् अनूत साईकुन् ?
I am a clerk	मैं एक कलर्क हूं
anna kaateb	अन्ना कातिब
am I a clerk ?	क्या मैं कलर्क हूँ ?
hal anna kaateb ?	हल् अन्ना कातिब ?

Some other interrogatives
(कुछ अन्य प्रश्नसूचक)

what	क्या	ayyeh	अय्यिह
when	कब	emtaa	इमता
where	कहां	ween	वीन
why	क्यों	leysh	लियश
which	कौन सा	eeh	ईह
who	कौन	meen	मीन

English	Hindi	Arabic	Pronunciation
how	कैसे	keef	कीफ
how many	कितने	cham	चम
how much	कितना	kaam	काम

Some verbs of daily use
(कुछ रोज़ प्रयोग में आने वाली क्रियाएँ)

English	Hindi	Arabic	Pronunciation
abandon	छोड़ना	yatrok	यतरक
abolish	खत्म करना	yobtil	युब्तिल
abridge	संक्षिप्त करना	yakhtasir	यख्तसिर
abuse	गाली देना	yoheen	युहीन
accept	मानना	yaqbal	यकबल
accompany	साथ जाना	yorafiq	यराफिक़
accustom	अभ्यस्त होना	ya'tad	यअ्नाद
acknowledge	पहुँच देना	yoqirr	युक्रिर
acquire	प्राप्त करना	yanal	यनाल
act	काम करना	yatasarraf	य-त-सर्रफ़
add	जोड़ना	yodeef or zad	युज़ीफ़ या जाद
admire	प्रशंसा करना	yo'jab	युअ्जब
admit	मान लेना	yaqbal	यब्बल
affirm	दृढ़ता से कहना	you'aqqid	युअ्क्क़िद
agree	मानना	youafiq	युवाफ़िक़
aid	साहयता करना	yousa'id	युसाम्रिद
allow	अनुमति देना	yasmah	यस्मह
amuse	खुश करना	yousally	युसल्ली
answer	उत्तर देना	youjawib or	युज्ञाबिब

		jawab	जबाब
pply	प्रार्थनापत्र देना	yatlob	यत्लुब
ppoint	नियुक्तकरना	youa'in	युअप्यिन
pproach	पहुँचना, समीप होना	yaqtarib	यक्तरिब
rrange	प्रबन्ध करना	youratib	युरतिब्र
rrive	पहुँचना	yasil or	सियल या
		wasal	वसल
sk	पूछ्ना	yas'al or	यस्सिल या
		sahal	साहल
ssist	सहायता करन	vou a'id	युसा'त्रिद
stonish	चकित करना	yandahish	यन्दहिश
ttach	साध लगाना	allaqa	अल्लका
ttract	आकर्षित करन	yajthib	यज्जिव
waken	जगाना	saha	साहा
ack	सहायता करना	yad'am	यद्अम
ark	भूंकना	yanabaha	यनबहा
athe	नहाना	yastahim	यस्तहिम
elieve	विश्वास करना	yousaddiq or	युसद्दिक् या
		saddak	सद्दाक
elong	सम्बन्ध होना	yakhoss	यखुस्स
lame	दोष लगाना	yaloom	यलूम
less	आशीर्वाद देना	youbarik	युबारिक
oil	उबालना	yaghli	यग्ली
orrow	उधार लेना	yasta'eer	यस्तअ्रीर
ow	झुकना	yanhany	यनहनी
reathe	सांस लेना	yatanaffas	य-त-नफ़्फ़स
ury	दफ़न करना	yadfin	यद्फ़िन

call	बुलाना	younady	युनादी
care	ध्यान करना	yatany	यञ्रतनी
carry	उठाना	yahmil	यहिमल
change	बदलना	yaughair	यग़य़ियर
cheat	धोखा देना	yaghosh	यगुश्श
claim	दावा करना	youtalib	युतालिब
clean	साफ़ करना	younathiff	युनाथिफ़
close	बन्द करना	yaqfil	यक़्फ़िल
collect	जमा करना	yajmah	यजमाञ्र
command	हुक्म देना	yamur	यञ्रमुर
complain	शिकायत करना	yashtaki	यश्तकी
complete	पूरा करना	yokmil	युक्मिल
confess	अपराध स्वीकार करना	yatarif	यञ्रतरिफ़
consider	विचार करना	yatabir	यञ्रतबिर
consist	शामिल होना	yashtamil	यश्तमिल
consult	परामर्श करना	yoshavir	युशाविर
contain	रखना	yahtawee	यहतवी
continue	जारी रखना	yotabch	युताविञ्र
cook	पकाना	yatabbak	यतबाञ्व
copy	नक़ल करना	yansakh	यन्सख़
correct	ठीक करना	yousallih	युस्लिञ्ह
count	गिनना	yaod	युञ्रद
cross	पार करना	yabor	यञ्रबुर
cry	चीखना	yasrokh	यसरूख़
dance	नाच करना	yarqoss	यर्क़ुस
deceive	धोखा देना	yakhda	यख़्दञ्र
decide	फ़ैसला करना	yoqarrir	युक़रिर
delay	देर करना	yata-akhar	यत-ञ्रख़्खर

depart	चला जाना	gadara	गादरा
deserve	योग्य होना	yastahiq	यस्तहिक्त
desire	इच्छा करना	yarghab	यर्गब
die	मरना	yamout	यमूत
digest	हजम करना(पचाना)	yahdim	यहिदम
dine	दावत देना	akal	अकाल
disappear	गायब हो जाना	yakhtafi	यख्तफी
discover	पता लगाना	yaktashif	यक्तशिफ़
dislike	नापसन्द करना	yakrah	यकरह
distribute	बांटना	yowazzih	युवज्जिग्न
divorce	तलाक	tallaqa	तल्लाक्त
do	करना	amal	अमल
doubt	आशंका करना	yashuk	यशुक
drink	पीना	shirib	शिरीव
dry	सुखाना	younashiff	युनशिफ़
dye	रंग करना	yasbogh	यस्बुग़
earn	कमाना	yaksab	यक्सब
emigrate	देश छोड़ना	youhajir	युहाजिर
employ	नौकर रखना	youwathif	युवाथिफ़
encourage	वढ़ावा देना	youshajiih	युशजिग्न
enter	भीतर जाना	yadkhol	यद्खुल
examine	जांच करना	yafhas	यफ़हस
excuse	बहाना बनाना	yathor	यथ्रथोर
explain	बिवरण देना	yashrah	यश्रह
fail	असफल होना	yoqassir	युक्रिसर
fear	डरना	yakha	यखाफ
feed	भोजन करना	wakkel	बाक्कील
fght	लड़ना	hareb	हरीव

finish	खत्म करना	yonhi	युन्ही
fold	तह करना	yatwi	यत्वी
follow	पीछा करना	yatba	यत्बम्र
forget	भूल जाना	nesi	निसी
free	छोड़ देना	atlaqa	अतलका
fry	तलना	yaqli	यक्ली
gain	फ़ायदा उठाना	yaksab	यक्सब
gamble	जुआ खेलना	yokamir	युक़ामिर
gather	जमा करना	yajma	यजमम्र
give	देना	gibu	गिबु
go	जाना	raah-yerooh	राह यिरू
hate	नफ़रत करना	yakrah	यक्रह
have	रखना	ah-indi	अाह-इन्दि
hear	सुनना	simi-ah	सिमी-अाह
heat	गर्म होना	yosakhin	युसख़िन
help	मदद करना	yosaid	युसाअिद
hire	किराए पर लेन	yastajir	यस्ताजिर
hit	वार करना	darab-yedreb	दरब-यिदरिब
hunt	शिकार करना	yastad	यस्ताद
hurry	जल्दी मचाना	asraa	असरा
inform	सूचना देना	youlim	युअ्लिम
inherit	अधिकार में पाना	yarish	यारिस
insult	अपमानित करना	yo heen	युहीन
interfere	दखल देना	yatadakhal	यतदाख़ल
interpret	अर्थ समझना	tarzeem	तरजीम
invent	अविष्कार करना	yakhtanih	यख़्तरिम्र
invite	दावत देना	yadoo	यद्म्रू
jump	छलांग मारना	yaqfiz	यक़्फ़िज़

kill	मार डालना	yaqtul	यक़्तुल
knock	दरवाजा खटखटाना	yaqra	यक़रह्र
know	परिचित होना	ah-arif	आह-अ्ररिफ़
laugh	हंसना	yazh-hak	यजहक
lead	मार्ग प्रदर्शन	yaqood	यक़ूद
leap	कूदना	yaqfiz	यक़िफज
leave	छोड़ देना	tarak	तारक
lie	झूठ बोलना	yakthib	यकथिब
lift	उठाना	yarfa	यर्फ़ह्र
live	रहना	yaeesh	यईश
look	देखना	yanzur	यन्ज़ुर
love	प्यार करना	hobb	होब
make	निर्माण करना	ah-amal	आह-अमल
marry	शादी करना	yatazawaj	यत-ज़व्वज
meet	भेंट करना	kabil	कबिल
mend	मरम्मत करना	yoslih	युस्लिह
miss	खो देना	awiz	अविज
mix	मिलाना	yamzij	यम्ज़िज
move	कारवाई करना	yataharrak	यतहर्रक
notice	ध्यान देना	yulahiz	युलाहिज
obey	हुक्म मानना	yotee	युतीअ्र
obtain	प्राप्त करना	nala	नाला
occupy	अधिकार करना	yosh ghil	युशिग्ल
offer	पेशकश करना	yoqaddim	युक़द्दिम
open	खोलना	yaftah	यफ़्तह
order	हुक्म देना	yamur	यम्रमुर
pack	वण्डल बांधना	hazam	हाजम
paint	रोगन करना	dahanu	दहानु

pay	वेतन देना	dafa-yedfa	दफा-यिदफा
permit	आज्ञा देना	samah	समाह
place	रखना	wadaa	वदा
play	खेलना	yalab	यलब्रब
prefer	अधिक मानना	yofadhil	युफदहिल
print	छापना	yatbah	यतबब्र
promise	वायदा करना	yaid	यग्निद
pull	खींचना	yajur	यजुर
push	धकेलना	yadfish	यद्फ़िश
read	पढ़ना	kara	कारा
receive	प्राप्त करना	yastalim	यस्तलिम
refuse	मना करना	yarfudh	यर्फुद
register	दर्ज करना	sogar	सोगार
remember	याद रखना	eftekar	इफ़्तीकार
remind	याद दिलाना	yojakir	युज्निकर
renew	नया करना	yojaddid	युजिद्दिद
repair	मरम्मत करना	sallah	साल्लाह
repeat	दोहराना	yokarrir	युकर्रिर
reply	जबाब देना	yojawib	युजाविब
resign	इस्तीफ़ा देना	yastakil	यस्तकील
respect	सम्मान करना	yahtarim	यहतरिम
rest	आराम करना	yatrah	यर्ताह
return	वापिस करना	yaood	यहूद
revolt	विद्रोह करना	yathoor	यथूर
ring	घंटी बजाना	yadoq	यदुब्क
rise	उठना	yanhaz	यनहज्ञ
rub	रगड़ना	yafrok	यफ्रूक
run	भागना	egri	ऐग्री

save	बचाना	youwafir	युवफ़िफ़र
say	बोलना	kal	काल
see	देखना	shu	शुफ़
seek	तलाश करना	dauwar	दौवार
sell	बेचना	baa	बा
send	भेजना	khud	खुद
serve	सेवा करना	yakhdim	यख़िदम
sew	सिलाई करना	yakheet	यख़ीत
shave	दाढ़ी बनाना	halak	हलाक
shout	चिल्लाना	yasrokh	यस्रूख
show	दिखाना	warra	वरा
shut	बन्द करना	kafal	काफल
sign	हस्ताक्षर करना	yowaqih	युवक़िक्ष्र
sit	बैठना	kahd	काहद
sleep	सोना	nam	नाम
smell	सूंघना	yashum	यशुम
smok	धुआँ देना	youdakhi n	युद्ख़िन
speak	बोलना	Itkallim	इतकानिम
stand	खड़े होना	yaqi?	यक़िफ़
start	चलना	safir	सफ़िर
stay	रहना	yabqa	यब्क़ा
stop	रुकना	yakoff	यकुफ्फ
store	जमा करना	yakhzin	यख़िज़न
study	पढ़ना	darass	दारस
succeed	सफल होना	yanjah	यन्जह
swim	तैरना	am	ग्रम
alk	बातें करना	yatakallam	यतकल्लम
ake	लेना	khod	खोद

taste	स्वाद लेना	yajook	यजूक
teach	पढ़ाना	ye-alem	यी-आलीम
thank	धन्यवाद	shakara	शकरा
think	विचार करना	eftekar	इफ्तीकार
threaten	धमकी देना	youhaddid	युहद्दिद
tie	बाँधना	yarbit	यर्बित
touch	छूना	yelmis	यीलमील
translate	अनुवाद करना	yetargem	योतारजीम
travel	सफर करना	yessafir	येसाफ़िर
trim	ढंग से सजाना	yektah	यीक्ताह
trust	भरोसा करना	yasiq	यसिक़
try	कोशिश करना	yajarrib	युजर्रिब
understand	समझना	fahim	फ़ाहिम
use	इस्तेमाल करना	yastamil	यस्तामिल
visit	मिलने जाना	yazoor	यज़ूर
wait	प्रतीक्षा करना	yantathir	यन्तथिर
walk	चलना	yemshi	यीमशी
want	चाहना	yoreed	युरीद
wash	धोना	yaghassil	यग़स्सिल
watch	चौकसी रखना	yoraqib	युराक़िब
weigh	तोलना	yazin	यज़िन
whisper	काना-फ़ूसी करना	yahmiss	यहिमस
wish	इच्छा करना	yarghab	यर्ग़ब
work	काम करना	yishtagha	यिशतागाल
wrap	लपेटना	yaliff	यलिफ़
write	लिखना	yakteeb	यकतीब

Lesson 6

Numbers

अंक

Cardinal (साधारण अंक)

Hindi/Arabic	*English/Arabic*
जीरो, शून्य	zero
सिफरी या सिफ़र	sifre **or** sifer
एक	one
वाहिद	wahed
दो	two
इतनैन (थनेन)	Ithnan (thnayn)
तीन	three
थलाथीह् (तलैता)	thalatheh
चार	four
अरबअाह्-आ	arba-ah-a
पाँच	five
खमसा	khamseh
छैं:	six
सितीह् (सित्ता:)	sitteh (sitta)
सात	seven
साब-आह्-आ (सबआ:)	sab-ah-a
आठ	eight
थीमानीह् (थमानिया)	themanieh

नौ	nine
तिस ग्राह-ग्रा (तिसाम्र:)	tis-ah-a
दस	ten
ग्राह-ग्राशरा (ग्राशरा)	as-ashra
ग्यारह	eleven
हदा ग्राह ग्रा (हिदाशर)	hada-ah ash
बारह	twelve
थना ग्राह-ग्राश (इतनाशर)	thna ah-ash
तेरह	thirteen
थलाता-ग्रा-ग्राश (तलाताशर)	thalata-ah-ash
चौदह	fourteen
ग्ररबा-ग्राह-ता-ग्राह-ग्राश (ग्ररबाताशर)	arba-ah-ta-ah-ash
पन्द्रह	fifteen
ख़ामस्ता-ग्राह-ग्राश (ख़ाम्सात्ताशर)	khamsta-ah-ash
सोलह	sixteen
सित्ता ग्राह-ग्राश (सित्ताशर)	sittah-ta-ah ash
सत्तरह	seventeen
साबी-ग्राह-ता-ग्राह-ग्राश (साबात्तशर)	saba-ah-ta-ah-ash
ग्रठारह	eighteen
थोमान्ता-ग्राह-ग्राश (थमनत्ताक्षर)	thomanta-ah-ash
उन्नीस	ninteen
तिसि-ग्राह-ता-ग्राह-ग्राश (तिसा: ताश)	tisa ah ta-ah-ash
बीस	twenty
ग्राह इशरीन (ग्रशरीन)	ah ishreen
इक्कीश	twenty-one
वाहीदो-इशरीन (वःहिद व ग्रशरीन)	waheedo-ishreen

बाईस	twenty-two
याह्-थनायनो-अशरीन (इतनैन व अशरीन)	ah-thnayno-ishreen
वगैरह	etc·
इला आखिरिहि	Ilah-ah-akhi-rihi
तीस	thirty
थलातीन (तलातीन)	thalatheen
चालीस	forty
अरब-ग्राह-इन (अरबईन)	arb-ah-een
पचास	fifty
खामसीन	khmaseen
साठ	sixty
सित्तीन	sitteen
सत्तर	seventy
साबाह-ईन	sab-ah-een
अस्सी	eighty
थोमानयीन	thomanyeen
नब्बे	ninety
तिस-ग्राह-ईन (तिसायीन)	tis·ah·een
सौ	one hundred
मो-ग्राह-ग्राह (मिया)	me-ah-ah
एक सौ एक	one hundred and one
मी-ग्राह-ग्राह-वाहीद	me-ah-ah-wahed
एक सौ दस	ond hundred and ten
मी-ग्राह-ग्राह-व-अशर:	me-ah-ah-wa-ashra

एक सौ तीस	one hundred add thirty
मी-ग्राह्-ग्राह्-व-थलातीन	me-ah-ah-wa-thalateen
बगौरह	etc.
इला ग्राखिरिही	Ilah-ah-akhirihi
दो सौ	two hundred
मियातैन (मी-ग्राह्-ग्रतायन)	me-ah-atayan
तीन सौ	three hundred
थलाल-मी-ग्राह्-ग्राह्	thalath me-ah-ah
चार सौ	four hundred
ग्ररबी-ग्राह्-मी-ग्राह्-ग्राह्	arbe-ah-me-ah-ah
पाँच सौ	five hundred
ख़म्स-मी-ग्राह्-ग्राह्	khams me-ah-ah
छ: सौ	six hundred
सित: मी-ग्राह्-ग्राह्	sita-me-ah-ah
ग्राठ सौ	eight hundred
थोमान मी-ग्राह्-ग्राह्	thoman-me-ah-ah
नौ सौ	nine hundred
तिसी-ग्राह् मी-ग्राह्-ग्राह् (तिस्म्र मिम्र:)	tise-ahm-e-ah-ah
एक हज़ार	one thousand
ग्रल्फ़	alf
दस हज़ार	ten thousand
ग्राह्-अशरत-ग्रा-ग्राह् ग्रल्फ	ah-ashrat a-ah-alf
बीस हज़ार	twenty thousand
इशरीन ग्रालाफ़	Ishreen-ah-alf

| दस लाख | one million |
| मिलयून | milli-uon |

Ordinal Numbers
क्रमानुसार

तर्तीबी अदद	Ordinal number	अल-आदा दुत्तर्तीबिया	
पहला	first	अल अव्वल	al-awwal
दूसरा	second	अथानी	athani
तीसरा	third	अथालीथ	athaleth
चौथा	fourth	अरंबी-आह	arrabe-ah
पाँचवा	fifth	अ न खमीस	al-khames
छठा	sixth	अग सदीस	as sades
सातवां	seventh	अस सबी आह	as sabe ah
आठवां	eighth	अथामीन	athameu
नवां	ninth	अत तसी आह	at tase ah
दावां	tenth	अल-आशिर	al-ashir
ग्यारहवां	eleventh	अल-हादी अशर	al-hadi asher
बारहवां	twelfth	अस सानी अशर	as sani asher
बगैरह	like that	इला-आखिरिही	Ilah-ah-akhirihi
बीसवां	twenteith	अल डशरीन	al-ashreen
पचीसवां	twenty fifth	अल-खामिस वल डशरन	al-khamees waal-ashreen
तीसवां	thirtieth	अल सलासीन	al salaseen
चालीसवां	fourtieth	अल अरबीयन	al-arb-aheen
पचासवां	fiftieth	अल खमसीयन	al-khamseen
साठवां	sixtieth	अस सित्तीन	as sitteen
सत्तरवां	seventieth	अस सबायीन	as-sab-ah-een

अस्सीवां	eightieth	अस थमानीन	as-thomanyeer
नव्वेवां	ninetieth	अस तीसायीऩ	as-tis-ah-een
सौवां	hundredth	अल-मी-ग्राह-ग्राह	al-me-ah-ah
हज़ाहवां	thousandth	अल-अल्फ़	al-alf
दस लाखवां	milionth	अल-मिलयून	al- miliuon

Fractional Numbers
भिन्नात्मक संख्या

कसरी अरदवें	Collective Fractional Numbers	अस्माउल जमा वल अादाउल कसरीय	
आधा	one half	नुस्फ़	nussf
तीसरा	one third	थिल्थ	thilth
चौथाई	one fourth	रुबी-ग्राह	rube-ah
तीन चौथाई	three fourth	थिलासुत अर्बास	thita-ah-sut-arbas
पांचबां हिस्सा	one fifth	खुम्स	khums
छठा हिस्सा	one sixth	सुद्स	sudas
सातवां हिस्सा	one seventh	सुबअ्र	su-ab-ah
आंठवां हिस्सा	one eight	थुमन	thuman
नवां हिस्सा	one nineth	तिसअ्र	tisa
दसवां हिस्सा	one tenth	उअ्र	asher
दर्जन	a dozen	दजीना	dazeena
आधा दर्जन	half-a-dozen	निस्फ़ दस्ता	nisf-dasta
एक कोड़ो, बीस	a score	इशरीन	Isheen
जोड़	a pair	ज़ौज	zoj
1988	1988	अल्फ वा तिसी-	alf-wa-tise-ah
		ग्राह-मी-ग्राह	me-ah-ah wa-

		आह व धमानिया	thamnia wa
		व थमानीन	thamaneen
सफ़ा पेज़ 55	55	सफ़हाख्म्सा व	safha-khamsa
		ख़मसीन	wa khamseen
नम्बर 270	270	रकम ाय रामगु	rag-um-me
		मी आह अता-	ah-atayan wa
		यान व सबायीन	sabaheen
दोहरा	double	ज़ोफ़	zof
तेहरा	triple	थलासूत-अज़ा-	thala-ah-sud-
		आफ़	ah-aaf
चारगुणा	fourfold	अर्ब अतु	arba-ataha
		अज़आफ़	zaaf
पांच गुणा	fivefold	ख़्म्सतु अज़आफ़	khamsa-tu-
			ah-ahzaa
छः गुणा	sixfold	सित्तत अज़आफ़	siteitu-a-
			aaf
दस गुणा	tenfold	अश्रतु अज़-	ashra-tu-az-
		आफ़	aaf
सौ गुणा	hundredfold	मी आह आह तु	me-ah-ah tu
		तु जअफ़	zaa-af

Lesson 7

Greetings & Time
शुभकामना और समय

Greetings	Fitta.hiaʒe
शिष्टाचार	**फिहतीय**
good morning	sabah el-khair
शुभ प्रभात	सबाहिल खैंर
good afternoon	assad allah auqat kom
शुभ मध्यान	अस अदल्लाहु औक़त कुम
good day	ta-aba-you mkum
शुभ दिन	ता-ब-यौ मकुम
good evening	masael khair
सांयकाल की नमस्ते	मसाईल खैंर
good night	tose-vee-ha ala khair
शुभ रात्रि	तोस्बीह-अला-खैंर
good luck	hazzan sayidan
अच्छी किस्म (अल विदाअ)	हज़्ज़ान सइदान
hello	assalama likum
नमस्ते, प्रणाम, सलाम	अस्लामा लिकूम
hello	wa-alaykum assalam
उत्तर :—नमस्ते	वा-अलेकम असलाम
good bye	fi amanellah bikha-atirak
खुदा हाफ़िज़	फ़ि-अमानील्लाह बिखातरिक

good bye :answer :—
उत्तर :—

ma-ah-assalameh
मा-ग्राह-ग्रस्सालामीह

cheer you
ग्रलविदाग्र

wida-ahyan
विदायन

see you again
फिर मिलेंगे

arra-k-sanniya-tan
ग्ररा-क-सानियतन

so long
ग्रल विदाग्र

illal-lieka
इलल-लिका

how are you ? (mas)
तुम्हारा क्या हाल है ? (पुल्लिंग)

kaeyfae haelik
कैयफै हेलिक

how are you ? (f)
तुम्हारा क्या हाल है ? (स्त्रीलिंग)

eshlo-anakh
ईशलोग्रानरव

very well, thank you
ग्रंच्छा है। शुक्रिया

bekheir, shukran
बिखेंर शुक्रन

I am fine
मैं ठीक हूँ ।

bkhair or
al-hamdulillah
बखें या ग्रल-हामदु
लिल्लाह

what is your name ?
तुम्हारा क्या नाम है ?

Isas muk-ay
इस्समुक ऐ ?

my name is Seema
मेरा नाम सीमा है

anna ismi Seema
ऐना इस्मी सीमा
or Ismi Seema
या इस्मी सीमा

where have you been ?

तुम कहाँ रहे हो ?

ein kont ?

ऐन कुन-त ?

I have not seen you for a long time

मैंने लम्बी मुद्दत से तुम्हें नहीं देखा ।

lamara-ka munaj mudat in-ta-wilatan

लम ग्ररा-क मुन-ज मुद्दतिन

तवीलतन

who are you (m) ?

ग्राप कौन है ?

(पुल्लिग)

meen enta

मीन ऐन्ता

how is your family ?

ग्रापके परिवार का क्या हाल हैं ?

Ishloan eli-ah-al ?

इशलोग्रान इली-ग्राह-ग्राल

every one is fine.

सभी ठीक है ।

shukaram kulu kuais

शुक्रन कुलु-कुग्राइस

I had headache and stomach ache

मुझे सर दर्द ग्रौर पेट दर्द की जिकायत थी ।

kan-mai-waja ras wa mida

का-न मग्रि-य वज-अ बिरीसि व बि-मिग्रद :

I am better today

ग्राज मैं ग्रच्छा हूँ ।

ana ashan el yaum

ग्रना ग्रहसनुल योम

how are your children

ग्रापके बच्चे कैसे है ।

eshloan awladekah (f)

इशलोग्रान ग्रावलादीख (स्त्रीलिग)

eshloan awladek(m)

इशलोग्रान ग्रावलादीक (पुल्लिग)

who are you ? (f)

ग्राप कौन है ?

meen enti

मीन ऐन्ति

I am an Indian or American tourist	ana-sayeh hindi or amrecani
मैं एक भारतीय या अमरीकी यात्री हूँ	अना-सायेह हिन्दी या अमरीकनी
may I introduce Mr (पुल्लिंग)	agaddemlak essayed ?
	आगद्दीमलाक इस्समीद ?
may I introduce (f) (स्त्रीलिंग)	agaddemlakh essayed ?
आइये मैं आपको इनसे मिला दूं ।	आगद्दीमलाख इस्सयीद ?
I am very pleased to meet you Mr, Miss or Mrs.	taesharafna essayed al-aniseh or essayida.
मैं आपसे मिलकर बहुत खुशी हुआ हूँ श्रीमान कुमारी या श्रीमति	तैशरफैना ईस्सयीद, अल-अनिसेह या ईस्सयिदा
what is your profession ?	shinhu shighlek (m)
आप कौन सा कार्य करते है ।	शिन्हु शुग़लीक (पुल्लिंग)
	shinhu shighlekh (f)
	शिन्हु शुग़लीख (स्त्रीलिंग)
I am a lawyer	ana muhami
मैं एक वकील हूँ	अना मुहामि
I am a clerk	ana katib
मैं एक क्लर्क हूँ	अना कातिब
watchman	muraqib
चौकीदार	मुराकिब
teacher (m)	mudarres or mo'allem
प्रध्यापक	मुदर्रिस या मुअल्लिम
tearcher (f)	mudarreseh
प्रध्यापिका	मुदर्रीसीह

merchant or business man	tajer
दुकानदार या व्यापारी	ताजीर

jewller	jawhary
जौहरी	जौहरी

engineer	muhandice
इंजीनियर	मुहन्दिसे

doctor	tabeeb
डाक्टर	तबीब

civil servant	mwadhaf hukumeh
सरकारी नौकर	मवादफ़ हुकुमीह़

carpenter	najjar
बढ़ई	नज्जार

dentist	tabeeb asnan
दांतो का डाक्टर	तबीब अस्नान

pharmacist	sayedali
कम्पाऊडर या दवाईयों की दुकान वाला	सायेदलि

please to have met you	tkharrafna bimariftak
आपसे मिलकर बहुत खुशी हुई ।	त्खाराफ़ना बिमारिफ़ताक

I'll see you tomorrow at home. so long	sa'arak ghadan fill beitk illa alliqa
कल तुम्हारे घर आऊंगा तब तक के लिए इजाज़त	स अ़रा-क गदन फ़ी बैतिक इल्लिका

I hope we shall meet again	hal itammel nij time-ab marra thanieh
मुझे उम्मीद है कि हम फिर मिलेंगे	हाल ईताम्मील निजतिमीआह़ मारा थानि1ह़

Days of the Week
सप्ताह के दिन

The parts of the day	*Akssam-ul-yaum* .
midnight	nisful-layl
आधी रात	निस्फुल्लैल
night	layl
रात	लैल
evening	masa-ah
शाम	मसाह
sun set	guru-ub bashamsi
सूरज डूबने का समय	गुरूबुशम्सि
mid day	nisf-unn-ah-har
आधा दिन	निस्फुन्नहार
noon	zuhr
दोपहर	जुहर
morning	sa·ba-ah
सुबह	सबाह
sunrise	tuloo-ah-al-shams
सूरज निकलने का समय	तलू-आ-अल-शमस
dawn	fajra
सुबह, प्रभात	फ़ज्र

The Days af the Week	*Ayyam Et Usbouh*
Sunday	al ahad
इतवार	अल-अहद

Monday	al athnayn
सोमवार	अल अथनायन
Tuesday	athalathe-ah
मंगलवार	अथालाथी-आह
Wednesday	al arba'a
बुधवार	अल-अर्बआ
Thursday	al khamees
वीरवार	अल खमीस
Friday	al-jum·ah
शुक्रवार	अल-जुमा
Saturday	as-sabt
शनिवार	अस सब्त

Seasons
मौसम

मौसम	फुसूलुस्सन	*Fusu-ulu-ussna-ah*	seasans
सर्दी, जाड़ा	इश शिता	Ish-shita	winter
पतझड़	इल खारीफ	el khareef	autumn
वसन्त	इर-रा-बी	Ir-rah-bee	spring
गर्मी	इस-सयफ	Is-sayf	summer

Months of the year
वर्ष के मास

साल के महीने	अश्हरूस्सन:	*Ashru-as-san*	The manths of the year
जनवरी	या नायिर या कानून थानी	ya nayer or kanoon thany	January

फ़रवरी	शब्बात या फ़िब्रि यिर	shbaat or fibri-yer	February
मार्च	मारीस या ग्रा-ग्राह-थर	ma-ris or a-ah-thar	March
अप्रैल	नीसान या ईव्रील	nissan or ibreel	April
मई	मायु या अय्यर	mayu or ayyar	May
जून	योनियाह या हज़ीरान	yone-yah or hozeiran	June
जुलाई	योलिया या तमूज़	yo!e-yah or tammouz	July
अगस्त	ग्रा-रोस-तोस या ग्राब	ar-ross-tos or aab	August
सितम्बर	ऐलूल या सिपतिम्बिर	aylool or Siptimbir	September
अक्तूबर	तिशरीन अव्वल या ग्रोकतोबिर	tishreen awal or actober	October
नवम्बर	तिशरीन थानी या नोवीम्बर	tishreen thany or noveember	November
दिसम्बर	कानून अव्वल या दीसीम्बीर	kanoon awal or deeceembeer	December

Time
समय

समय	ख्ज़-ज़मन	*Azz-zan an*	*Time*
सैकिन्ड	सानिय	sa-ah-nceya	a second
मिनट	दक़ीक़ा	dakika	a minute
दस मिनट	अशरा दक़ीक़ा	ashrah dakika	ten minutes

आधा घण्टा	निस्फ़ से त्रैं	nisf sae ae	half-an-hour
घण्टा	सा-ग्राह	sa-ah	an hour
दिन	यौम	yaum	a day
हफ़्ता	उस्बूह	osbooh	a week
पन्द्रह दिन	उस्बूग्रान	osboo-an	a fortnight
महीना	शहर	shahr	a month
साल	साना	sana	a year
सदी	क़र्न	quarn	a century
समय कंसे बताया जाता है ?	कैं-फ़ तक़ूलुज वक़-त	*Kaif takool el wakt*	*How to tell time*
क्या समय हुआ है ? या कितने बजे हैं	इसा-ग्र कम या ईस्सा-ग्राह-ग्रा चम	Is-sa-a-kam *or* Iss-ah-a cham	what time is it ?
साढ़े सात बजे हैं ?	ग्रस-सा ग्रा ग्रस-साबि ग्रा विनस्स	as-saa-ah as-saabiah win uss	half past seven
बारह बजे हैं ।	ईस्सा-ग्राह-इस्नाअशर	Issa-ah-Isna-ah-shar	It's 12 o clock
आठ बजे हैं ।	ईस्सा-आह-ग्राथामिना	Iss-ah-atha-mina	It's 8 o' clock
साढे बारह बजे हैं	इस्सा इस्ना-ग्रा शर व नुस्फ़ ग्रह इस्ना ग्रा-शर	Issah-isna-ah shar-wa nusf ah-isna-ah-shar	half past twelve
सवा बारह बजे हैं ।	इस्सा-ग्र-शर व रूबी ग्राह	Issa-h-Isna-ah shar wa-rubeah	quarter to twelve

12 बज कर 10 मिनट हुए हैं	इस्ना-प्र-शर-व प्राशरतु दकीक	Isna-ah-shar wa ashratu dakeek	It is ten minutes past twelve
12 बज कर 5 मिनट हुए हैं ।	इस्ना प्रशर व खमुस दकाइक	Isna-ah-shar wa khamus dakaeek	It is five mintues past twelve
सात बज कर बीस मिनट हुए हैं ।	साबाह प्रो-प्राह थिल्थ	sab-ah-o-ah thilth	twenty minutes past seven
नौ बजने में बीस मिनट बाकी है ।	प्रस-साप्र तुत्ता सिप्रतु इल्लाथिल्थ	assa-ah-tuta-si-ah-tu illa-thilth	It is twenty to nine
पाँच बजने में 15 मिनट बाकी है ।	खाम-सा इल-ला रोब	kham-sa-il-la rob	quarter to five
पौना एक बजा है (एक बजने में 15 मिनट हैं)	इस्सा वाहिद इला रूबा प्रह	Issah waheed-illa-rube-ah	quarter to one
एक बजा है ।	इस्सा प्रा-प्र वाहिद	Issa-ah-a waheed	It is one o' clock
छः बज कर बीस मिनट हुए हैं	सित्तीह प्रो प्राह-थिल्थ	sitteh o-ah-thilth	twenty past six
साढे दस बजे हैं ।	प्रशरा प्रोह-प्राह नुस	ashra o-ah-nus	half past ten
दोपहर	ईदीहीर या इदुहर	edheher **or** edhuhr	noon
दोपहर के बाद	प्राह-प्रसर	ah asr	afternoon

थोड़ा वक़्त	बुर्हा	bur-a-ah	a while
लम्हा	लहज़	la-ha-za-ah	a moment
देर	मुतअख़िर	muta-ah-khir	late
जल्दी जल्दी	इघरे-इघरे	Ighrae-ighrae	quickly
जल्द	बाकिरन	ba-ha-kiran	early
ठीक समय पर	फिल मेविद	fil-maewid	in time
आज	अल-योवम	alyowm	today
आने वाला कल	बुखरा या गदन	bukhrah or ghadan	tomorrow
गुजरा हुआ कल	अल बारिह या अम्स	al-bari-ah or ams	yesterday
आज रात	अल-लयला	al-laylah	tonight
आधी रात	नस फ लयल	nus f-layl	midnight
पिछला साल	अस-सनतुल माज़िय या इससाना इल-ली फातित	as-sannatul maziah or Issa-na-il-lee-fatet	last year
परसों (बीता हुआ)	अव्वलु अम्स	awalu ams	day before yesterday
पिछला महीना	इश-शाह रि इल-लीफत या अश-शहरुप माज़ी	Ish-shah-reil-lefat or ash-shahrul mazi	last month
अगला महीना	अश-शहरूल क़ादिम	ash-shahrul kaadim	next month
आने वाला हफ़्ता	अल-उसबूअूल कादिम	al-osbooh-ul ka-adim	next week
आने वाला साल	अस सनातुल कादिमा	as-sann-ah-tul-ka-adima	next year

हर साल	कुल-ल सनः	kula-al-sann-ah	every year
हर महीने	कुल-ल शहर	kul-al sha-ahar	every month
प्रतिदिन	कुन-ल यौम	kul-al youm	every day
रोज़ाना	यौमी	yaumi	daily
हर सप्ताह	कुल ल-उस्बूत्र	kul-al osbooh	every week
सालाना	सनबी	sanvi	yearly
मासिक	शहरी	shahri	monthly
साप्ताहिक	फ़िल उस्बूत्रः	fil-osbooh	weekly
एक साल में	फ़िस्सनः	phis-sanna-ah	per year
एक दिन में	फ़िल यौम	fil-yaum	per day
एक हफ्ते में	फ़िल ल्स्बूत्र	fil-osbooh	per week
एक महीने में	फ़िश-शहर	phish-sha-har	per month
पिछली रात	इल-ले ला इलली फ़ातित	el-lay-la-il-lee fatit	last night
दिन	इन ना हार	In-nah-hahr	the day

Weights and Measures

भार और नाप

वज़न (नाप तोल)	वज़न	*Wazan*	*Weight*
			(The metric system is in use)
ग्राम	घ्राम	ghram	gram
सौ ग्राम	मी-घ्राह-घ्राह घ्राम	me-ah-ghram	100 gram
दो सौ ग्राम	मी-घाह-घ्रतायन घ्राम	me-ah-atayan ghram	200 gram
हज़ार ग्राम या किलो	किलो	kilo	1000 gram or kilo

पाँच सौ ग्राम (आधा किली)	खम्स-मी-आहू-ग्राह ग्राम था निस्फ़-किलो	khams-me-ah-ghram or nisf kilo	500 gram (half a kilo)
चौथाई किलो (250 ग्राम)	रूबाग्र-किलो	rubeah-kilo	one fourth of a kilo (250 gms.)
एक पाउण्ड	रितील	ritel	one pound
मीटर	मिट्र or मीटर	mitr or metre	metre
किलोमीटर	किलोमीटर	kilometre	kilometre

Asking for things
कुछ मांगना

कैसे ?	कैफ़ ?	kaif ?	how
कहाँ ?	वायेन ?	wayn ?	where ?
कौन ?	मीन्हो ?	menhow ?	who ?
मुझे चाहिए ।	आ-ग्राह ताज	a-ah-taj	I need
क्या ?	शीन्हो ?	shenhow ?	what ?
कुछ और	खलास	khalaas	anything else
अभी नहीं	बग्रद	ba'ad	not yet
मैं वहाँ कैसे पहुंच सकता हूँ ?	ईशलोग्रान अ-ग्राह ग्रागदार, ग्रोसाल हनक	eshloan-a-ah agdar osal hnak ?	how can I get there?
मैं नहीं जानता	इहन्ना मिश ग्रार-फ़ीन	eh-nah mish ahr-feen	I don't know
यह क्या है ?	शीन्हु हाथी ?	shenhu hathe ?	what is this ?

वह क्या है ?	ऐ दा ?	ay da	what is that ?
मुझे चाहिए क्यों ?	आ-आहरीद लेश ?	a-ah-reed laysh ?	I want why ?
हम कहां जा रहे हैं ।	ईह-ना री-होन फेन	eh-nah ri-heen fayn	where are we going ?
कल तुम कहाँ थे ?	ईन कोनता अल-बारि-आह ?	ein konta al-ba-ariha ?	where were you yester-day ?
वह कहां है ?	वायेना ?	wayna ?	where is it
मैं क्या करूं ?	आ-मिल ए	ah-mill-ay	what am I to do ?
कब ?	मता ?	mata ?	when ?
वह कहाँ हैं ? (स्त्रीलिंग)	वायनहीय ?	whaynhey ?	where is it (f)
क्या तुम्हारे पास आह-इन्दख ? है ? (स्त्रीलिंग)		ah-indak ?	have you (f)
कभी नहीं	मुत्लक्न, अबदन	motlaqan, abadan	never
क्या हुआ ?	ऐश सार	aysh sar ?	what has happened ?
क्या तुम्हारे पास आह-इन्दक ? है ? (पुल्लिंग)		ah-indak	have you (m)
क्यों नहीं	लेश इतगोअल	laysh etgoalah ?	why not ?
कितने का है ? या क्या कीमत है	इशगाद या चाम	eshgad or cham	how much ?
यह स्त्री कौन है ?	मीन्तील मरा हाथी या मीन्हीय ?	menteel mara hathi or menhey ?	who is this lady ?

श्रापके पिता कहाँ है ?	ईन श्रबूक ?	ein abook ?	where is your father ?
वह श्रादमी कौन हैं ?	मीन्हो या मीन मरा हाथी ?	menhow or meen mara hathi ?	who is this man ?
सबसे नज़दीक बाज़ार कहाँ है ?	श्रैयनै श्रकरब बज़ार ?	aeynae akrab bazar ?	where is the nearest bazar ?
क्या तुम्हारे पास कोई सिगरेट हैं ?	ईन्दक सका इर ?	Indak saka ir ?	do you have any cigar-ette ?
यह कितने का है ?	बिकैम	bikaem	how much is it ?
क्या यहाँ मेरी कोई चिट्ठी है ?	फी लकतूब लो ?	fee maktoob lee ?	is there any letter for me ?
क्या रात के खाने का इन्त-जाम है ?	हसत श्रकिल हूनी	hast akil hnee ?	is the din-ner ready
क्या यहाँ पर सिनेमा है	फी सिनेमा	fee sinama	is there any cinema here ?
शायद	रूबमा	robama	perhaps

Four Directions
चार दिशाएं

दिशाएं	अल-जिहातुल अर्बअ	*Al-Jihat ul arba*	*Directions*
पूरब	अश-शर्क	ash-sharq	east
पश्चिम	इल-गारब	el-gharb	west
उत्तर	अश शिमाल	ash-shimal	north
दक्षिए	अल जुनूब	al-janoub	south

Lesson 8

Phrases in Common Use
साधारण वाक्यांश

मुझे भूख लगी है (पुल्लिंग)	I am hungry (m)
जु-आह-आन	ju-ah-an
मुझे उम्मीद है ।	I hope
बा-आह-अम्मील	ba-ah-ammel
मुझे अकेला छोड़ दो ।	leave me alone
खाल्लिनि	khallini
मुझे भूख लगी है (स्त्रीलिंग)	I am hungry (f)
जुआह-आनीह	ju-an-anoh
तुम बहुत दयालु हो ।	you are very kind
फ़दलक आह-अलैना	fadlak ah-alaina
तुम गलती पर हो ।	you are wrong
अनता गलतन	anta ghaltan
मुझसे मत पूछो ।	don't ask me
ला तास अलनि	la tas alni
मैं भूखा नहीं हूँ ।	I am not hungry
आना लास्तो जाईह	ana lasto jaeh
मैं समझ गया ।	I understand it
फ़हाम्त	fahamt

वह क्या है ? — what is that ?
ऐ दा ? — ay dah ?

मैं नहीं जानता । — I don't know
इह्ना मिश ग्रार-फीन — eh-nah mish ahr-feen

मैं विश्वास करता या करती हूँ । — I believe so
हाल्लून वा-ग्राह्-तिगीद — halloon ba-ah-tiged

मुझे देर हो रही है । — I am late
त-खारत या मिताखीर — t-khart or mitakher

इसमे कोई फ़र्क़ नहीं पड़ता । — It doesn't matter
उन्ना माहली — unna mahlee

हो सकता है ऐसा हो । — It may be so
योम्कीम थालेक — you.nkim thalek

मैं कुछ नहीं समझा । — I don't understand
मोश फ़ाहेम — mosh|fahem

कोई बात नहीं । — never| mind
मा-ग्राह-ग्रालाइह — ma-ah-alaih

फिर मिलेंगे । — see you again
अरा-क सानियतन — ara-k saniytan

डाकखाने में । — at the post-office
फी मक्तबिल बरीद — fi maktibil bareed

सचमुच — of course
लाज़ीम — lazeem

ऐसा मत कहो । — don't say so
ला ताकुल हकादा — la takul hakadha

मुझे अफसोस है ।	**I am sorry**
आना आसिफ़	ana asif
आपका स्वागत है (स्त्रीलिंग)	**you are welcome** (f.)
आह-ईलाफ़ो	ah-elafow
कृपया बैठ जाओ ।	**do sit down**
त्फादल इखीथ राहतीक	tfadhal eketh rahtek
आप वहाँ कैसे जाते हैं ?	**how do you go there ?**
आ रूह-हि-नाक इज़-ज़ी ?	ah-rooh hi-nak iz-zi ?
चलो चलें ।	**let's go**
याल्ला खाल इन्रूह	yalla khal in rooh
नहीं ।	**no**
लाह	lah
इसका उत्तर था जवाब यह है ।	**the reply is**
हादरीन **या** मकानीक	hadhreen **or** makanek
हाँ	**yes**
ना-आह-आम **या** ईह	na_ah-am **or** eeh
यहाँ इन्तज़ार करो ।	**wait here**
ईस्तुन्नाह हीन्नाह	issutunah hennah
कृपया बहुत धीरे बोलिए ।	**please speak more slowly**
मिनफिदलक कुल्लीम बीशवेश	min fidlak kullem besh waysh
देखो (स्त्रीलिंग)	**look** (f.)
चुफ़े **या** शुफ़े	chufay **or** shufay
मुझे दिखाइए ।	**let me see it**
दह्नी अराहा	dahnee araha

इस जगह का क्या नाम है ? what is the name of this place?

अय-इस्सम ईल-माहुल्ल दी ? ay-essm el-mahull dee

भागो run

इदकीद या इदबीच (पुल्लिंग) irkedh or idbech (m)

इरकदे या दिब्चे (स्त्रीलिंग) irkdhay or dibchay (f.)

कृपया please

मिन फ़ादलीक (पुल्लिंग) min fadhlek (m.)

मिन फ़ादलीरब (स्त्रीलिंग) min fadhlekh (f.)

यह जरूरी है । this is necessary

हादि दरूरियाह hadi drurieyah

मेरे लिए टैक्सी बुलाओ । call me a taxi

हात-आहलि तीक्सी hat-ahli texi

अभी बहुत जल्दी है । it is still early

लेलहीन फ़ि-वग्त lail-heen fi-wagt

(तुम, स्त्रीलिंग) थोड़ी देर रुको (you f.) wait a while

ओह-आह-गाफ़े कालील o-ah-gafae kaleel

मेरे पास समय नहीं है । I have no time

मा लि वक्त ma li waqt

इतनी देर तक so long

इलल लिका elal lika

रास्ता दिखाइए lead the way

इमिश जिद्दामि imish jiddhami

आपको शुक्रिया (धन्यवाद) thank you

शुक्रन shokron

वे मुझे हर रोज देखते हैं ।	they see me everyday
याज़ूरूनी कुल्ल यौम	yazurunee kull youm
बिल्कुल कुछ नहीं	nothing at all
ला शाए अबादन	la shai abadan
कृपया कीजिए	please take
त्फादल	tfadhal
सुना	listen
इस्माह	essmah
अन्दर आओ	come in
तफादल या इदखोल	t'adhal or edkhol
ये महँगे है	these are inexpensive
हादि अरखास	hadi arkhas
सफलता प्राप्त करो	come to success
हि आ-ला अल-फा-ला	hi-ah-lah al fah-lah
क्या आप इसको ठीक कर सकते हैं ?	can you mend this ?
ओरिद रेफ़ित हैज़े मिन फदलक	orid raeffit haezae min fadlak
मुझे बीच में मत बुलाओ	don't interrupt me
ला तक़ता कलामी	laa taqta kalaamee
मुझे क्षमा कीजिए	excuse me
एस्माहलि या आह-ईलाफ़ो	esmahli or ha-elafow
मैं केवल पूछने के लिए आया या	
आई हूँ	I came just to enquire
अटायट लिल इसटी लाम	atayt lil istee lam
यह कब तक तैयार हो सकता है ?	when will it be ready ?
मीते ते तेकून गेह्रिजे ?	maetae tae tackun gachizae ?

मेरी चाबी गुम हो गई है ।	I have lost my key
मुफ़ताही दा-आ	muftaahee daa-ah
तुझे आज इसकी जरूरत है ।	I need it today
ओरिदग्रोऐ ग्रेल योम	oridohae ael yom
मैं क्षमा मांगता या मांगती हूँ	I apo'ogize
बा-हा तिथिर-आतिथिर	ba-ha tither atither
(तुम, पुल्लिग) थोड़ी देर रुको ।	(you, m.) wait a while
ओ-ग्राह-गाफ़ कालील	o-ah-gaf kaleel
कृपया आप कष्ट मत कीजिए (पुल्लिग)	don't trouble yourself please (m).
ला तित-ग्राह-इब-नाफ़सीक	la-tit-ah eb-nafsek
मुझे यह सुनकर अफसोस है ।	I am sorry to hear it
आसिफ़ लिसिमाग्नि हाज़ा	asif lisimaea haza
रुको (स्त्रीलिग)	stop (f)
ओ-ग्राह-गफ़ें फे	o-ah-gfay
मुझे ठीक तरह अरबी बोलनी नहीं आती ।	I don't speak Arabic well
ना ग्राह ई तीकाह्लम अरबी ज़न	ma ah-ee tekallam arbi zain
तुम्हें अरबी सीखनी चाहिए ।	you should learn Arabic
आहलेक ग्रान तात-हह्लाम ग्रल-रबी-ग्राह	ahlaik an tat-hallam al-arbee-ah
तुम्हें लिखूंगी	I will write to you (f)
नाकतिव्लाख	bakti blakh
रुको (पुल्लिग)	stop (m.)
ओ-ग्रा-गाफ़	o-ah-gaf

क्या आपके पास माचिस या सि.रेट है — have you any matches or cigarettes

आहन्दुक कुब्रीत वीह सुग्गिगीर ? — ahnduck kubreet weh suggighe

कृपया अन्दर अइये (स्त्रीलिंग) त्फ़ादलि — please come in (f) tfadhali

मेरा इन्तजार कीजिए । इन्तज़िर नी — wait for me Intzer nee

देखो (पुल्लिंग) चुफ़ — look (m) chuf

मैं तुम्हें लिखूंगा बाकतिब्लाक — I will write to you (m) bakti black

कृपया अन्दर आइये (पुल्लिंग) प्फ़ादल — please come in (m) tfadhal

वहाँ पर कोई तौलिया नहीं है । मब्फ़ीश फ़ूता — there is no towel muffesh foota

तौलिया दराज (शेल्फ) के ऊपर पड़ा है । तानम फ़ी इल्बाशकीर नाला रफ़ — the towel is on the shelf nanam fee ilbashkeernala ra

यह बुरा है (पुल्लिंग) हाथी-आह मोब ज़ेन — this (m) is bad hathe-ah mob zain

मेरे पीछे आओ इत्बा-इनि (स्त्रीलिंग) इत्बानि (पुल्लिंग) — follow me Itba-eeni (f) Itabni (m)

आपके (या तुम्हारे) पीछे वा-.राह-दक-आेगबाक — after you ba-ah dak ogbak

रवि बोल रहा है ।
रवि यतकल्लम
Ravi is speaking
Ravi yatakallam

चले जाम्रो ।
रूह याललाह
go away
rooh yallah

यह बुरी है (स्त्रीलिंग)
ह्ाथीय मोब जेनीह
this is bad (f)
hathey mob zaineh

मैं शर्मिन्दा हूँ ।
मति-म्राह-म्रास्सीफ
(पुलिंग)
I am sorry
meet-ah assef (m)

वह भूठा है ।
हुवा कद्दाब
he is a liar
huwa kadhdhab

मेभे म्रपना पता दो (स्त्रीलिंग)
म्रातिनि-म्राह-इन्वानीख
give me your (f) address
atini-ah-inwanekh

कृपया यह तुम लिख दो ।
एकतिबलि याह मिन फ़ादलीख
(स्त्रीलिंग)
please write it down
ektibli yah, min ſadhalekh (f)

इकतिब्ली याह मिन फ़ादलीक
(पुलिंग)
Iktiblee yah, min ſadhlek
(m)

जल्दी करो (स्त्रीलिंग)
ज़ितात या हामी या म्राज्जले
hurry up (f)
zitat or hami or ajjlay

मुभे यह देखने दो ।
दाहनि म्रराहा
let me see it
dahni araha

मुभे समभ में यह नहीं म्रा रहा ।
मा फ़हम्त
I don't understand it
ma ſahamt

जाओ और उसे बुला के लाओ (पुल्लिंग)	go and call him
रूह ना-दीह	ruh-na-deh
मुझे आज्ञा दो ।	allow me
इस्माहिलि (स्त्रीलिंग)	Ismahili (f)
इस्माहलि (पुल्लिंग)	Isma hli (m)
मैं शर्मिन्दा हूँ (स्त्रीलिंग)	I am sorry (f)
मीत-आह-अस-आह-फाहि	meet-ah-as-ah-feh
जल्दी करो (पुल्लिंग)	hurry up (m)
ज़ितात या हामी या आज्जील	zitat or hami or ajjel
मुझे अपना पता दो (पुल्लिंग)	give me your (m) address
आतनि आह-इन्वानीक	atni ah-inwanek
उसे बताओ	tell him
कुल लु	qul lu
मुझे बताओ	tell me
खाब्बीरनि	khabber ani
तुम्हारा टेलीफोन नम्बर क्या हैं ? (स्त्रीलिंग)	what is your telephone number ? (f)
चाम निम्रत टेलीफ़ोनीख	cham nimrat 'elephonekh ?
मुझे नहीं मालूम है ।	I don't know
मा-आह-अर्फ़	ma-ah-aerf
मुजे मालूम है।	I know
आ-आह-अर्फ	a-ah-arf
ढूढना (पुल्लिंग)	look out (you m)
दीर बालीक़	deer balek

कृपया तुम मेरी मदद करो (पुल्लिंग)	help me please (you m)
सा आह इदनि	sa-ah-idni
चुप हो जाओ ईहदा	be quite ihda
बैठो मत ला तक़हुद	don't sit la taqhud
मैं आपके लिए क्या कर सकती हूँ ? ऐश तोऊलीन ओह-आह-मोरी हादरीन	what can I do for you (f) aish tgouleen o-ah-mori hadreen ?
तुम्हारा टेलिफोन नम्बर क्या है ? (पुल्लिंग) चम निम्रत टेलीफ़ोनीक ?	what is your telephone number (m.) cham nimrat telefonek ?
ढूंढना (स्त्रीलिंग) दीरि बालेख	look out (you, f.) deeri balekh
मैं आपके लिए क्या कर सकता हूँ ? ऐश ग़ोऊल ओ्रो-आह-मोरी हादरीन ?	what can I do for you ? (m.) aish tgoul o-ah-mori hadreen ?
खिड़की बन्द करो (तुम पुल्लिंग) बान्नीद-दिरिशी-आह	shut the window (you, m.) banned-dirishe-ah
कृपया तुम मेरी मदद करो (स्त्रीलिंग) सा-आह-दीनि	help me (you, f.) sa-ah-deeni
आपका स्वागत है (पुल्लिंग) तिक़्रम या आह-इलाफ़ो	you are welcome (m.) tikram or ah-elafow..
खिड़की बन्द करो (तुम स्त्रीलिंग) बान्दि-दिरिशी-आह	shut the windnw (you, f.) bandhi-dirshe-ah

जाओ और उसे बुला के लाओ (स्त्रीलिंग)	go and call her (f.)
रूह नाद-आह-ही-आह	ruh-nad-ah-he-ah
सच बात बताओ ।	tell the truth
कुलिस-सुदक्	qulis-sudq
रात का खाना तैयार है	dinner is ready
अल-आहशा हादिर	al-ahsha hadir
मैं नहीं विश्वास करता या करती ।	I don't believe it
आमा मा सादीग	ama ma saddeg
मैं तुम्हारा स्वागत करता या करती हूँ	I welcome you
आहलान वा साहलान	ahlon wa sahlan
आराम से बैठिए	make yourself comfortable
स्फादलि इखीथि राहतीख	tfadhali ekhethi rahtekh
मुझे देखो (तुम, पुलिंग)	look at me (you, m.)
ईत्ताल्ली-आन-इनि	ittalle-ah-ini
यह रंग नहीं रहेगा	this colour won't stand
हाथा अल्लून ला यादून	hatha alloun la yadoon
दया करो (स्त्रीलिंग)	have (f.) the kindness
सा-आह-दिनि	sa-ah-dini
अभी चले जाओ (स्त्रीलिंग)	Go away, now (f)
अल-आह-हीन तिस्माही त्रोऊहीन मिन हनी	Al-ah-heen tismahi troheen min hnee
मुझे देखो (तुम, स्त्रींग)	Look at me (you, f)
इत्ताल्ली-आह-इनि	Ittalle-ah-ini
आपकी अतिथि सेवा के लिए धन्यवाद	Thank you for your hospitalit
इन्शाऊला दायमीह	Inshalla daymeh

आज कौन सा दिन है?	what day is to day?
मा अल-यौम ?	ma al-youm ?
मुझे दिखाओ (स्त्रीलिंग)	show me (f.)
बचौऊफ या रांबीनि	bachouf **or** raweeni
मुझे धन दो ।	give me the money
'जिब ली इस-फूलूस	jib lee is-fuloos
दया करो (पुल्लिंग)	have (m) the kindness
सा-आह-इदनि	sa-ah-idni
अभी चले जाओ (पुल्लिंग)	go away, now (m)
अल-आह-हीन तिसमाह त्रौऊहीन	al-ah-heen tismah trouh
मिन हनी	heen min hnee
मुझे दिखाओ (पुल्लिंग)	show me (m)
बचौऊफ या राबनि	bachouf **or** raweeni
मैं तुम्हारा धन्यवाद करता हूँ (पुल्लिंग)	I thank you (m)
अशकुरक	ashkurak
मैं कुछ कपड़े खरीदना चाहता हूं ।	I want to buy some clothes.
ओरीडो एन ऐसटारी कुईमाशग्रन	oreedo an ashtari qimashan
यह अच्छा है (पुल्लिंग)	this (m) is good
हाथी-आह-जेन	hathi-ah-zain
मैं परवाह नहीं करता ।	I don't care
ला उबालि	la ubali
मैं तुम्हारा धन्यकाद करती हूँ ।	I thank you (I, f)
अशकुरख	ashkurakh
यह अच्छी है ।	this (f) is good
हाथीख जेनोेह	hatheekh zaineh

मैं क्या करू ?	what am I to do ?
आ-मिल ए ?	ah-mill ay ?
तुम बहुत लम्बे हो	you are very tall
ऐन्ता तबील जिद्दन	enta taweel jiddan
यह मेरी गलती नहीं है ।	it is not my fault
मिश-राल तित-ती	mish-rahl-tit-tee
क्या तुमने मुझे समझ लिया था ? (पुल्लिग)	did you understand me ? (m)
हाल फ़हाम्त मां गील्त ?	hal fahamt ma gelt ?
कृपया मेरे लिए क्षमा माँग लो (स्त्रीलिंग)	please apologise (you, f) for me
मिन फादलीख इ-ग्राह-तिथिरिलि	min fadhlekh i-ah-tithrili
मैं थका हुआ हूँ ।	I am tired
ता-ग्राह-बानीह (स्त्रीलिंग)	ta-ah-banieh (f)
ता-ग्राह-ग्रबान (पुल्लिग)	ta-ah-aban (m)
कृपया मेरे लिए क्षमा माँग लो (पुल्लिग)	please apologise (you,m) for me
मिन फ़ादलीक इ-ग्राह-तिथीरलि	min fadhlek i-ah-titherli
कृपया ग्रपने ग्रापको दुखी मत कीजिए (स्त्रीलिंग)	please don't trouble your self (f)
ला तित-ग्राह-इबी नाफ़सीख	la tit-ah-ebe nafsekh
दरवाज़े को खट खटाओ	knock at the door
दुक्क-ग्रल-बाब ग्रसलिफ़ीन	duqq-al-bab aslifni
सावधान रहिए (स्त्रीलिंग)	Be careful (you f)
ख़ालि बालीख़	khali balekh

मुझे जाना है ।	I must go
लाजीम ग्रम्शी	lazeem amshi
मुझे दो	give me
ग्रातनि	atni
मैं नहीं दे सकता	I cannot pay
ग्रना ला ग्रकदर ग्रदफा	anna laa-aqdar adfa

Lesson 9

Customs and Baggage
शुल्क और यात्रा का समान

सीमा शुल्क दफ़्तर कहाँ है ?	whene is the customs house ?
फ़यन-इल-गुम रुक ?	fayn-el-gum ruk ?
आपका समान कहाँ है ?	whene is your luggage ?
ऐ-न अम्ति़अतुक ?	ein amti atuk ?
यहाँ अनुमति पत्र, यात्रा	here is the passport,
का समान है ।	and baggage
ग वाज-इस-सा फार सुमम-व	gawaz-is-sah-fahr
इल-आफश आ-होह	sum-mum wa el-ahfsh ah-hoh
क्या ये थैले आपके हैं ?	are these bags yours ?
हल हाथी ही अल हकाइबुलक ?	hal hathi hi al haqah-ibu lak ?
यहाँ बीसा और प्रमाणपत्र है ।	here is the visa and identifi-
इत्ता-शीरा सुमम-व इल-बिता	cation card
-आ ईश शख-सीया आ होह	et-ta -sheera sum-mum wa el-
	betah-ah ish-shakh-seeya ah-
	hoh
क्या ये सन्दूक आपके है ?	are these trunks yours ?
हल हाज़िहिश शुनतु लक ?	hal hazihish shuntu lak ?
हाँ	yes
ना-आह-आम -	na-ah-am

नहीं	no
लाह	lah
क्या आप मेहरवानी करके इन्हें खोलेंगे ?	would you open these please ?
इफतह हाथींहि मिन फादलीक ?	iftah hathihi min fadlik ?
खुशी से जनाब	with pleasure, sir
बिकुल्लि सुरूर या सय्यिदी	bikul soroor ya saidi
आपके पास कुछ घोषित करने के लिए है ?	have you anything to declare ?
अनदाक हाजात मिन अल-मम नू आत ?	andak haajaat min al-mum noo-aat ?
क्या आपके पास ऐसी चीज़ है जिस पर ड्यूटी लग सके ?	do you have anything to pay duties for ?
हल मअक शैय लितदफ़ अलैंहि जुम्रूक ?	hal maak shai litadfa aleihi jumrook ?
मेरे पास घोषित करने के लिए कुछ नहीं है ।	I have nothing to declare
मम आ यीश-हा गा आले-हा गुम रुक	mam-ah-yeesh-ha ga ahlay-ha-gum ruk
कोई मना की हुई चीज़ ?	anything forbidden ?
हल मिन शैइम मम्नूअ ?	hal min shai mamnooh
कुछ और ?	anything else ?
खलास ?	khalass ?
मेरे पास यही कुछ है ।	that is all I have
दा कुल इल-ली मे इ-या	da kul illee may-i-yah
मेरे पास सिर्फ़ मेरे कपड़े है ।	I have anly only my clothes
मम्री मलाविसी फ़क़त ।	mai malabi si faqat

मैं समान का निरीक्षण कहाँ कर सकता हूँ ।	where can I check the baggage ?
अ-सल-लिमिश-शोह-नात्त फोन ?	a-sal-limish-shoh-naht fayn
सामान रखने का कमरा	the baggage room
ओ-दितिल ड्ल-ग्राफश	oh-ditel-ahfsh
कुली कृपया यह मेरे लिए ले जाओ	porter, please carry these for me
याशीयाल, मिन फादलक-शिल ली दोहल	ya-shi-yal, min fahdluk shel-lee dahl
इसे ध्यान से पकड़ो ।	handle this carefully
हासिब ग्रा-ज़ादी	hah-sib ah-lah dee
मैंने ग्रापको कितना देना है ?	how much do I owe you ?
ग्रा-बिज़ काम ?	ah-wizkam ?

Lesson 10

Directions

दिशाएँ

Hindi	Arabic	Pronoun	English
बाहर	बुर्रा	bur-rah	outside
अन्दर	गो-वा या दाख़ील	goh-wah **or** dakhel	inside
रास्ता	सिरात	sirat	way
दांयें को मुड़ो	खद् यामीनक	khudh yameenak	turm to right
जाओ	रूह	ruh	go
आगे	जिद्दम, उद्दाम	jiddam, youddam	in front of
यहाँ	इहनी आह	ihne-ah	here
शहर की तरफ	बिल ख़ारिज या बर्रा-आह	bil kharij **or** barra-ah	outside
पीछे	वरा, ख़ल्फ़	wara, khalf	behind
वहाँ	हुना-क	honak	there
दायें	यमीन	yameen	right
बायें	यीसार, शिमाल	yesar, shimal	left
बीच में	बेन	bain	between
परे	वरा	wara	beyond
दूर	बाहीद	bah-eed	far
नज़दीक	जिरीव, अारीब कुर्ब	jireeb, ahreeb, qorb	near

ऊपर	फ़ौक़	faoque	above
बीच में	खिलाल	khilal	among
सामने	मजाबील	mjabel	opposite
पहले	क़ब्ल	quable	before
नीचे	तहत या	taht **or**	down **or** below
	अस्फ़ल	asfal	
नीचे की तरफ	लितहत	litaht	downward
सीधा सामने	सीदी ग्राह	seede-ah	straight ahead
रास्ता दिखाश्रो	इमिश जिदमि	imish jiddami	lead the way
...कहाँ है ?	बेनी ईल	wayne el	where is the...

क्या यह सीधा रास्ता है ?
ही-या-दी सिक-कित

Is this the direct way to··· ?
hee-ya-dee sik-kit

क्या यह ठीक रास्ता है ?
ह्याथि तारीक़ इला ··?

Is this the right way to···?
hathi-tareq ill ?

क्या ग्राप मुझे······का रास्ता
बता सकते हैं ?
मुमकीन-इद्वालिनी ग्राह-ग्राला···?

would you direct me to... ?
mumken-iddalini ah ala ··?

कृपा करके मुझे रास्ता दिखाश्रो ।
मिन-फादलिक वानी नी इस-सिक
का (पुल्लिंग)

please show me the way
min-fahdlik wah-ree nee is-sikk
(m)

मिन फादलीख वा री नी इस-सिक
का (स्त्रीलिंग)

min-fadlekh wah-ree nee is-sikk
(f)

(वहाँ का)···छोटा रास्ता   which is the shortest way to
कौन सा है ?

(शिन्हु) या शिनो ब्रगसर तारीक़   (shinhu) or shinow agsar tareeq
(ली) या इला······?   (le) or ila···?

Lesson 11

Taking a Taxi
टैक्सी लेना

कृपया मेरे लिए एक टैक्सी मंगवा दें — please call a taxi for me
मिन फाद लक ना-दी-ली ताक-सी — min fahd-lak na-dee-lee-taksi

ड्राईवर क्या तुम खाली हो ? — are you free, driver ?
मा-ग्राह-इन्दक शे सव्वाक — ma-ah-indak shay sawwaaq

मैं एक होटल में जाना चाहता हूँ — I want to go to hotel
विद्दी-आ-ग्राह रुह-इल ओ-ग्राह तेल — waddi-a-ah ruh-il o-ah tail

किसी ग्रच्छे रेस्तरां में — to a good restaurant
इला-मत-ग्राह-ग्रम जेन — ialla mat-ah-am zain

ग्रमेरीकन ग्रमबैंसी की तरफ — to the American embassy
इला-सफरा ग्रल ग्रमरीक़ीया — illa-safara al Am-ree-kee-ya

क्या यह दूर है ? — Is it far ?
बाईद ? — baeed ?

मुझे ले चलो... — take me to ..
इखिथ-नि इला — Ikhith-ni ila ..

किराया कितना है ? — what is the charge ?
ग्रल-उजराह काम ? — al-ujrah kaam ?

समुद्र-तट का छोटा रास्ता कौन-सा है — which is the short way to the beach ?
ग्रय्यु नगैक हियन प्रमसरू इलल वनाज ? — ayu tarrek hiaal aqsar ila-al blaz ?

यहाँ से कितनी दूर है वह... how much to go from here to ..

चम ताखिथ मिन-इहनी-ब्राह cham takhith min-ehne-ah ila...?

इला__?

क्या पास है ? is it near ?

करीब qareeb

मुझे बन्दरगाह ले चलो take me to a harbour

विद्दी ग्रा-ब्राह-रूह इल ब्रो-मीनाह widdi-a-ah-ruh-ill o-meenah

कृपया धीरे चलाब्रो please drive slowly

मिन फाद लक सूब्रा-ला मा लक min-fahdluk soo-ah-lah mah-lak

यहाँ मेरा इंतजार करो wait for me here

ब्रो-ब्राह गाफ़ लि हनी o-ah-gaf li hnee

देरी मत करना don't be late

ला ता ब्रख खीर laa-ta akh kheer

ब्राब्रो हम चलें come on, let us go

इया बिना haya bina

मैं चाहता हूँ ब्राप मुझे दर्शनीय I want you to take me for sight

स्थानों का शहर में चक्कर लगवा दें seeing around the city

विद्दी ताखिथनि-हक ़फ़ारि्रजनि widdi takhithni-hak tfarrijni-ah-

ब्राह-ब्रलाल मदीनीह alal madineh

मैंने तुम्हें कितना देना है ? how much do I owe you ?

ा विज़ कम ? ah-wiz kam ?

Lesson 12

At the Hotal
होटल में

मैं एक अच्छा होटल चाहता हूँ लेकिन महंगा नहीं	I want a good hotel but not an expensive one
उरादु फुन्दुकन जय्यदन वलाकिन लैं-स गालिबन	oreedu fondocan jeiyedan wallaken leisa ghaliban
क्या आपके पास कोई कमरा हैं ?	have you any room ?
हल इन्दकुम ग़ुरफ़ ?	hal indakan ghoraf ?
क्या तुम्हारे पास बड़ा कमरा है ?	do you have a large room ?
हल इन्दक ओदह कबीराह ?	hal indak audah kaberah ?
मुझे दो बिस्तरों वाला कमरा चाहिए	I want a room with two beds
उरीदु ग़ुर-फ़तन बिसरी रैन	ourid ghorfatan bisari rayan
ग़ुमलखाने के साथ	with a bath room
बी हाम-माम	bec hahm-mam
कुहारे के साथ	with a shower
बी-दुश	bee-dush
वातानुकूलन कमरा	air-conditioned room
ग़ादामू की याफा	oh-dah moo-kee-yafa
आप एक दिन का कितना किराया लेते हैं	how much do you charge per day ?
काम तातलुब फ़ि-अ्रल-यौम ?	kam tatlub fi-al-yowm ?

मैं एक हफ्ते के लिए कमरा लूंगा	I shall take a room for a week or so
इद दी-नी ओ्रो-दा हा-वाली ओ्रोत बू	Id-dee-nee oh-dah hah-wahlee ohs-boo
एक रात के लिए	for one night
लि ले-ला वा-दा	~~li-lay-lah wah-dah~~
मुझे एक (सोने के लिए) कमरा दिखाओ्रो	show me a bedroom
ओ्रारिनि ओ्रौदत नौम	arini audat nowm
क्या इसमें टेलिफोन है ?	is there a telephone ?
हल यूजद हातिफ़ ?	hal youjed hatif ?
मैं यह कमरा लूंगा	I will take this one
ओ्राखुद हादि	ahkhud hadi
मैंने ओ्राज रात के लिए कमरा रिज़र्व कर रखा है	I have a reservation for tonight
ओ्र नाहा-गिज़ इल-ले ला दी(पुल्लिग)	a-nah-ha-giz el-lay-le-dee (m)
ओ्र ना हाग-ज़ा इल-ले-ला दी (स्त्रीलिग)	a-nah-hag-za el-lay-la-dee (f)
मेरे कमरे का नंबर क्या है ?	what is the number of my room ?
मा-हु-व रक़मु गुरफ़ती ?	ma houw raqmu ghorfati ?
मुझे मेरे कमरे की चाबी दो	give me the key of my room
ओ्राहतीनि मिफ़्ताह ओ्रौदाति	ah-teeni miftah owdati
मैं ओ्रपना कमरा बदलना चाहता हूँ यह बहुत छोटा है	I want to change my room it is too small
उरीदु ग़ैर गुफ़्ती इन्हा सग़ीरतुन जद्न	oreed gheir ghorfati inaha saghiraton jedan

क्या इस में लिफ्ट है ?	Is there a lift ?
हल यूजद मसअद ?	hal youjed masa ad ?
कमरा बहुत गर्म है	the room is too hot
इल श्रो दा हार	el-oh dah hahr
मैं गर्म पानी से नहाना चाहता हूँ ?	I want a hot bath
ब्राह-ब्रायिज हम्माम-सुखुन	ah-ayiz hammam-sukhn
मेरे लिए साबुन और तौलिया लाश्रो	bring me some soap and towel
यिब्रीलि (स्त्रीलिंग) यिबलि (पुल्लिंग)	yibeeli (f) yibli (m) sabun
साबुन विफवात	wifwat
मुझे एक और कम्बल दीजिए ।	give me another blanket
अ्रत्रतिनी हरामन ब्राजर	aatini hraman ahzhar
कृपया बिस्तर लगाईये ।	please make the bed
मिन फाद लिक रूतती बी इससि-रीर	min fahdlik rut li bee is se-reer
घण्टी किधर है ?	where is the bell ?
फैन ब्रल जारसं ?	fain al jaras
मैं कुछ खाना चाहता हूँ	I want something to eat
ब्रारीद शै लिल-ब्रक्ल	areed shai lil-aql
मैं अ्रपना नाशता अ्रपने कमरे में करना चाहता हूँ	I want my breakfast in my room
ब्र-नाह ब्रोव-जा इलफो तार फिल्ल ब्रो दाह (स्त्रीलिंग)	a-nah ahwiz elfoh tahr fil-oh-dah (f)
ब्र-नाह ब्रा-विज इल फो तार फिल श्रो या दाह (पुल्लिंग)	a-nah ah-wiz elfoh tahr fill oh-dah (m)

कृपया मुझे एक तकिया ला दो	please bring me a pillow
मिन फादलिक हा तीली में खुद दा	min fahdlik ha tee.ee may khud da
क्या मैं यह कीमती चीजें होटल में सुरक्षित रख सकता हूँ ?	can I leave these valuables in the hotel safe ?
श्राह-दार अ-सीब इल-हा-गात दी फिल्ल अमानत ?	ah-dahr a-seeb illah-gat dee fill ama-nat ?
मैं कब चैक करूँ ?	when must I check out ?
अ सीब इल श्रो दा इम ता ?	a seeb el oh dah emtah ?
क्या तुम्हारे पास मेरा कोई पत्र है ?	have you a letter for me ?
अन-दाक गाव-ब ली या ? (पुल्लिंग)	an-dak gah-wab lee yah (m)
अन-दिक गाव-ब ली-या ? (स्त्रीलिंग)	an-dik gah-wab lee yah (f)
मैं कल जाना चाहता हूँ	I am thinking of leaving to-morrow
अनवि अल दहाब बुकराह	anwi al dahab bukrah

Lesson 13

At the Restaurant
(रेस्टोरेंट में)

क्या यहाँ पर एक अच्छा रेस्टोरेंट है ? फी मात अम जैन ?	is there a good restaurant ? fee matam zain ?
आपका स्वागत है अहलन व सहलन	you are welcome ahlan wa sahlan
हमें मेज की आवश्यकता है । इह ना ओव जीन ता-रा बी जा	we need a table eh-nah ow zeen tah-rah bee-zah
आप कहाँ बैठना पसन्द करेंगे ? ऐन तुरीदु-न अन तज्लिसू ?	where would you like to sit ? ein toreedon an tajlisu ?
वहाँ कोने में हुना-क फ़िज्ज़ाविय	there in the corner hunnak fi azzawi
मेज रिजर्व है अल मेज माजूज़ा	the table is reserved al-maize mahjoozah
कृपया मुझे लिस्ट दीजिए आह-आतनिल लिस्टी-आह	please give me the list ah-atnil-liste-ah
कृपया मीनू लाइए लाइहतुत्त आम मिन फ़ज्लिक	the menu, please laihatu atta-am min fadlik
खुशी से जनाब बिकु लिल सुरूर या सयियदी	with pleasure, sir bikol soroor, ya sayedi

आप क्या चाहेंगे ?	what would you like to have ?
तिहिब्ब शू ?	tehibb shoo ?
हमें देखने दो, तुम्हारे पास क्या है ?	let us see what you have today ?
लिनरा मा था इन्दकुमुल यौम ?	linara matha indakom el yaum ?
मेरे लिए खाने को कुछ नहीं है	I don't have anything to eat
माफ़ि आह-ईन्दी शैं लिल-अक्ल	mafi ah-indi shai lil-akl
डबलरोटी और मक्खन लाओ	bring bread and butter
जीब खुब्ज़ बा जिब्दाह	jeeb khubz wa zibdah
मुझे मांस (मीट) अच्छा लगता है	I like the meat
अना बा-हीब इल-आह माह	anah ba-heeb el-lah mah
क्या यहाँ मछली है ?	is there fish here ?
यात्रा फि समक हुना ?	yatra fi samak huna ?
क्या यह ताजा है ?	is it fresh ?
इन कान ताज़ाह	in kan tazah ?
कृपया मेरे लिए···लाओ	please bring me······
मिन फदलक यिबलि···	min fadhlek yibli···
(a) शोरबा मुर्ग़	chieken soup
शोरबतु दजाज	shaurabatu dajaj
(b) उबले हुए अंडे	boiled eggs
बैजु मस्लूक	beiju maslouq
(c) आमलेट	omelet
इज्ज	ijj
(d) आलू कोरमा	potatoes stew
यख़िनतु बताता	yakhnitu batata

(e) साग — spinach
सबानिख — sbanikh

(f) बैंगन — egg-plant
बार्जिजान — bazinjan

(g) सुग्रर का गोश्त — pork
लहम खिन्ज़ीर — lahm khinzir

(h) आइसक्रीम — ice-cream
बौज़ा — bouza

(i) नींबू वाली चाय — tea with lemon
शयें बिलीमून — shai beleimon

यह मीट (मांस) जला हुआ है । — this meat is burned
इल-लाह मा दी माह-रू-अ — el-lah mah dee mah-roo-a

क्या सूप तैयार है ? — is the soup ready ?
हाल इल शोरबाह हादिराह ? — hal il shorbah hadirah ?

क्या यह पीने के लिए अच्छा है ? — it this good for drinking ?
हाल यसलाह लिल शुर्बु — hal yaslah lil shurb ?

मैंने इसके लिए आर्डर नहीं दिया — I did not order for this
अनी मा-ता लब्त हाथी-आह — aneh ma-talbat hathe-ah

क्या आपके पास अंग्रेजी बीयर है ? — do you have English beer ?
फ़ि आह-इन्दक बीरीआह इंगलिज़ी-याह — fi ah-irdak beeree-ah inglizi-yah

बोतल को खोलो — open the bottle
इफ़्ताह-इल-क़ान्निनाह — iftah-il-qanninah

कृपया चाय और केक लाओ — please bring tea and cakes
मिन फ़द्लक जीब शैं वकाहक — min fadhlak jeeb shai waqahaq

यह अभी कच्चा है	this is under-cooked
हाथी-आह मोब मिसतिवि	hathe-ah mob mistiwi
चटनी लाग्रो	pass me the sauce
नाविलनि-अल-मराक़ाह	nawilni-al-maraqah
एक तेज छुरी लाग्रो	give me a sharp knife
आतोन सिचीन क़ात-आहीह	atni sicheen qat-aheh
एक कप चाय और	another cup of tea
फ़िंजान शैं थानि	finjan shai thani
मेरी प्लेट बदलो	change my plate
गाय्हीर साहनि	ghayyir sahni
मैं कॉफी ला रहा हूँ	i am bringing coffee
अना जाया बिल काहवा	ana jaayan bilqahwa
यह ठण्डी है	this is cold
हाथी-आह बारीद	hathe-ah bared
मेरे लिए दूसरा लाग्रो	bring me some other
यिब्ली बा-आहाद वाहिद	yibli ba-ah-ad wahid
आज की विशेष डिश	today's special dish
इल इकलिल मख़ मूसाह अल योबम	el-iklil makhsoosah al yowm
खुशी के साथ जनाब	with pleasure, sir
बिकोन सोरूर या सायदी	bikol soroor ya sayadi
भोजन बहुत अच्छा था ।	the food was excellent
इल-अक-लि कन मोम-ताज	el-ak-li kan mom-taz
कृपया मेग बिल लाग्रो ।	please give me the bill
आह-आतनिल हिसाब मिन फ़ादलीक	ah-atnil hisab min fadhlek

बिल में गलती है ।   there is a mistake in the bill

फि रूल-ता फिल हि-साब   fee rul-tah fill he-sab

भान (खुले पैंसे) रख लो ।   keep the change

खाल ली इल-बा-ई ग्रा-ला शा नुक   khal lee ill-bah-ee ah-lah sha

(पुल्लिंग) निक (स्त्रीलिंग)   nuk (m) nik (f.)

ग्रापका घन्यवाद   thank you

शुक्रन   shukran

Lesson 14

At the Bank
बेंक में

The monetary unit is known as lira or dinar which is divided into one hundred units called piasters (like paisa in India)

अरब देशों में मुद्रा को लिरा या दीनार कहते हैं जो कि सौ भागों में विभाजित हो सकती है । इसे पिएस्टर कहा जाता है (जैसे भारत में पैसा कहते हैं ।

यहाँ कौन सा बेंक सबसे नजदीक है ? फेन ग्रा-रूब बंक हिना ?	where is the nearest bank here? fayn ah-rub bank hina
क्या ग्राप ट्रेवलर चेंक का भुगतान कर देंगे ? बितिस्रिफुन चीक़त सीयाहीयीह ?	do you cash traveller's cheques bitisrifun chekat siyahiyeh ?
मैं ग्रपना खाता खुलवाना चाहता हूँ । ग्रना ग्ररीद ग्रफता हिसाब	I want to open my account ana areed aftah hissab
क्या ग्राप मेरे चेंक का भुगतान कर देंगे ? बितिस्रीफ़लि चीक खास ?	can you cash a personal cheque bittisrifli ehek khas ?
मैं किस खिड़की से चेंक कैश करवा सकता हूँ । ग्रास-रिफ़ इश-शीक दा फेन ?	at which window can I cash this cheque ahs-rif ish-sheek da fayn

मेरे पास कुछ डालर हैं ।	I have some dollars ?
मा-ग्राहे या (इन्दी) दोलारात	ma-ahai **or** (indi) dolarat
डालर की विनिमय दर क्या है ।	what is the exchange rate of the dollar ?
इद-दो-लार बी-काम ?	id-doh-lahr bec-kam ?
मैं उनका भुगतान चाहता हूँ ।	I would like to exchange them
ग्रा-ग्राह-रीद ग्रा-ग्राह-सरीफ़ही-ग्राह	a-ah-reed a-ah-shrifhe-ah
कृपया इसे बदल दें ।	please change this for··
मिन-फादलक री-यार दोल ली	min-fadluk ri-yahr dohl lee
मैं कहाँ अपने हस्ताक्षर करूँ ?	where should I sign ?
ग्रैयने ग्रोवखि ?	aeynae owakki ?
एक पैसा (पिएस्टर)	one piaster
क़िर्श	qirsh
पाँच पैसे (पिएस्टर)	five piasters
ख़मसत कुरूश **या** तारिफ़ा	khamsat qurush **or** tarifa
दस पैसे (पिएस्टर)	ten piasters
ग्राह-ग्रशरत कुरूश	ah-ash-rat qurush
बीस पैसे (पिएस्टर)	twenty piasters
रिया-ग्र-ग्राल	riya-a-ah-al
पच्चीस पैसे (पिएस्टर)	twentyfive piasters
रूबी-ग्राह-लिरा **या** रूबा गिन्नी	rube-ah-lira **or** ruba ginni
पचास पैसे (पिएस्टर)	fifty piasters
नुस्फ़ लीरा	nusf lira
एक पौंड	one pound
गिन्नी **या** वाहीद गिन्नी	ginni **or** waheed ginni

Lesson 15

Post-Office
डाकखाना

नजदीक का डाकघर कहाँ है ?	where's the nearest post-office ?
श्रेयने अकरब मैकतेब बैरिद ?	aeynae akrab maektaeb bae-rid ?
डाकघर के खुलने और बन्द होने का क्या समय है ?	what time does the post-office open/close ?
मैंते येफतैह/यकफिल मैकतेब ग्रैल बैरिद ?	maetae yaeftaeh/yakfil maektaeb ael baerid ?
पैदल जाने के लिए यह काफी दूर है ।	It is too far to go on foot
इन्नहू बअ्रीद जिद्दन लिश्रन तश्ह-ब माशियन	Innahu baeed jiddan lian tathab mashiyan
मैं कहाँ से कुछ टिकट खरीद सकता हूँ ?	where can I buy some stamps?
ऐन युम्किननी अन अशतरी बश्रज्त्त-बाबिश्र	ein youmknuni an ashtari bazattah-wabeh ?
मुझे कुछ (टिकट) चाहिए ।	I want (stamps)
आ-आहरीद (ख्वाबी-आह)	a-ah-reed (twabe-ah)
पत्र	letter
मकतुब	maktub
कार्ड	[card]
बित्का या कार्त	bitqa or kart

मनी ग्राॕर्डर	moneyorder
हवाला-वरीदिय्या	hawaalah-bareediyyah
पोस्टल ग्राॕर्डर	postal order
हवालीह् बारिदियीह्	hawaleh baridiyeh
हवाई पत्र	air mail
बिल बैरिद ग्रैल गैव्वि	bil baerid ael gaewwi
टेलिग्राम (तार)	telegram
बरिक्यीह्	bariqiyeh
लिफाफा	envelope
जर्फि गवाव	zarfi gawaab
मैं एक तार भेजना चाहता हूँ	I want to send a telegram
ग्रन्न ग्रसीद ग्रब ग्रथ बरकिय्या	anna areed ab ath barqiyyah
कृपया मुझे तार भेजने का फार्म दे दें	please give me a telegram form
मिन फादलीक ग्रतनि वरागात	min fadhlek atni waragat
बार्किय्ीह्	barqiyeh
ग्रास्ट्रॆलिया (भारत) भेजने का प्रति	how much is per word to
शब्द क्या लेने हो ?	Australia (India) ?
चम इलकलमिह् इला ग्रस्तरालिया	cham ilkalmeh illa Ostralia
(ग्रलहिंद)	(al-hind)
मैं मनीग्राॕर्डर कहाँ से भेज सकता हूँ ?	where can I send a postal money order
ऐन युम्कि नुनी ग्रन ग्रसिल हवालतन	ein youmk nunce an orsil
वरीदीय ?	huwalatan bareedia ?
मैं यह पत्र भेजना चाहता हूँ	I want to send this letter
ग्रा-ग्राहरॆद ग्राह-रसील हल मकनुब	ah-ahreed ah-rasel hal maktub
या हाथिर्रिसालीह्	or hathirrisaleh

रजिस्ट्री कहां डाल सकता हूँ ?	where can I post a registered letter ?
...न युम्किमुनी ग्रन ग्रसिल रिसालतन ...मून ?	ein youmk runee an orsil risalatan mazamoun ?
कृपया यह पत्र रजिस्टर कर दीजिये	register this letter for me, please
...मिन फ़ादलीक साज्जिल्ली (हल ...कतुब) या हाथिर-रिसाली-ग्राह	min fadhlek sajjilli (hal maktub) or hathir risale-ah
इसे भारत रजिस्टर्ड हवाई-डाक से ...जना चाहता हूं	I want to send it by registered air mail to India
...ग्रा-ग्राररीद ग्रारस्लि-ई-ग्राह (पुंल्लिग) ...ग्रारसीलही-ग्राह-(स्त्रीलिंग) बिल ...रीद इव जाव्वी-इल-मुसज्जत इला ...ल हिंद	a-ah-reed arcile-ah (m) [arcilhe-ah (f) bill bareed il jawwi il-musajjat ela al hind
इस पार्सल को भेजता चाहती हूँ ...रिद इरसेल हेज़ेल तर्द	I want to send this parcel orid irsael haezael tard
...स पार्सल में क्या है ? ...नो फितार्द हाथी-ग्राह ?	what is in this parcel ? shinow fit-tard hathe-ah ?
...सके ग्रन्दर केवल पुस्तकें हैं ...फि गाईरिल-कतोब	there are only books inside ma-fi ghairel-kutob
...स पार्सल में टूटने वाली वस्तुएं हैं ...पया ध्यान रखें	this parcel is fragile, please be careful
...आह-ताब, मिन फ़ादलीक ख़ाल ...लीक	ye-ah-tab, min fadhlek khal balek
...सकी रसीद मुझे दे दें ...हतिनि बिहि वसल	give me a receipt for it ah-tini bihi wasl

मैं एक पोस्टल ग्राॅर्डर...(वहाँ) भेजना चाहता हूँ	I want to send a postal order to
ग्राहरीद ग्राह-ग्रारसोल हवालीह बारिदिगीह (इला) या लीग्राह	ah-reed ah-arcil hawaleh bar diyeh (ila) or le-ah
मैं भेजने वाला हूँ ग्राना-ग्रला-मुरांसिल	I am the sender ana-al-mursil
क्या ग्रापके पास रवि ांहब के नाम कुछ खत है? ग्रग्निन्द क रसाइल तहिमल इस्नुस्सच्यिद रवि?	have you any letters addresse to Mr. Ravi ? aindak rasae tahmil ism assayed Ravi ?
यह एक है हाथिही वाहिदा	here is one hathihi wahida
क्या ग्राप्के पास परिचय पत्र (शनाख्ती ग्राॅर्ड) है? हाल महाका हाविय्यैह?	do you have your ident caıd ? hal mah-aka hawiyeh ?
यह मेरा पासपोर्ट है हेज़ै पसपोरि	here is my passport haezae paspori

Lesson 16

The Apartment
मकान के विषय में

ं एक कमरे की तलाश में हूं।	I am looking for an apartment.
़ाना शा दोब वार ़ाला शा-श्रा	ah-nah shoh dob wahr ahlah sha-ah.
या श्राप के पास किराए के लिए ़ोई फ्लैंट है ?	have you an apartment to let ?
ल ब्रिन्द कुम शक़फ़ लिलई जार ?	hal indkum shaqf lili jar ?
़ं हमारे पास है।	yes, we have
़म ब्रिन्दना	na-am indana
़ोई घर के साथ	with a kitchen
़े मुत बाख	bee mut bakh
़सलखाने के साथ	with a bathroom
़ दि रित मी याह	bee dee rit mi yah
़ाने के कमरे के साथ	with a dining room
़ो ़ो दित सोफ़ रा	bee oh dit shof rah
कमरा देखना चाहता हूं।	I should like to see the room
़-दार श्र-शूफ़ इल-श्रो-दा	ah-dahr a-shoof el-oh-dah
या श्राप पहली मंज़िल पर चाहते है ़ दूसरी मंज़िल पर ?	do you want it in the first or second floor ?
़ तुरीदुहा फ़्ित्ताबिकिल श्रव्वल श्रम ़त्ताबिकिस्सानी ?	a turee doha fiatt-biqal awal am fiatta-biqis-sani ?

क्या आप फ़र्नचिर लगा हुआ चाहते है ?	do you want it furnished ?
अतुरीदुहा मफ़रूश ?	aturee-doha mafroosha ?
हाँ	yes
ना-आह-आम या ईह	na-ah-am **or** eeh
मुझे सामने वाला फ़्लैट चाहिए ।	I want a front apartment
उरीदु शक्क अमामीय	oreedu shaqqa amamia
मुझे देखने दांजिए ।	let me see it
दअनी अराहा	da ani araha
दरवाजे को ताला नहीं लगता ।	the door doesn't lock
इल बाब मा बीयि फिल्श	el bab ma bee ye filsh
क्या इससे भी कोई अच्छा है ?	have you something **better ?**
अनदाक हागा आह-सन ?	an-dak haga ah-san ?
किराया कितना है ?	what is the rent ?
कमिल ईजार ?	kamil ijar ?
क्या इससे भी कोई सस्ता है ?	have you a cheaper ?
अन-दाक हागा आर-खास ?	an-dak haga ahr-khahs ?
क्या नीचे भी कोई (कमरा) है ?	have you downstairs also ?
अन-दाक हागा हत ?	an-dak haga haht ?
क्या आपको एक साल के लिए चाहिए ?	do you want it for a year ?
हल तुरीदुहा लिसन ?	hal turee-doha lisana ?
हाँ (नहीं) ।	yes (no)
ना-आह-आम (लाह)	na-ah-am (lah)

Lesson 17

Travelling Agency
ट्रैवलिंग एजेन्सी

मुझे अफसोस है कि मैं आपको तकलीफ दे रहा हूँ ।	I am sorry to trouble you
अन्ना असिफ लिम-दि-ऐ-तक	anah asif lim-di-ay-tak
सबसे नजदीक ट्रैवलिंग एजेन्सी कहाँ हैं ?	where is the nearest travelling agency ?
ऐयने अकरब वकालतिस्सफ़री रात ?	aeynae akrab wakalati assafriya
नमस्ते (सुबह की) जनाब	good morning, sir
सबाहल खैर या सय्यिदी	sabahel kheir ya saidi
नमस्ते जनाब, क्या हाल है ?	good morning, how do you do?
सबाहल खैर कैइफ हालुक ?	sabahel kheir, keif haluk ?
कृपया बैठ जाईए	sit down please
त्फ़ादल ऊक्हुद	tafadhal uqhud
शुक्रिया (धन्यवाद)	thank you
शुक्रन	shukran
कोई सेवा जनाब	any service, sir
अयात खिदमां या सय्यिदी	ayat khidma ya saidi
क्या आप सफर करना चाहते हैं ?	do you want to travel ?
हाल तोरीद आन तोसाफ़िर ?	hal torred an to safir ?

हाँ, लेकिन अकेला नहीं	yes, but not alone
नाहम, वा लाकिन लेईसा वाहदि	naham, wa lakin leisa wahdi
परिबार के साथ	with my family
मग्र आइलती	ma ailati
आप कहाँ जाना चाहते हैं ?	where do you want to travel ?
इला एईन तीरोदोन असफ़र ?	ill ein toreedon ass a far ?
भारत, (पाकिस्तान, आस्ट्रेलिया)	India (Pakistan, Australia)
अल-हिंद (बाकिस्तान, अस्तरालिया)	Al hind (Bakistan, Ostralia)
आप कुल कितने लोग हैं ?	how many are you ?
माहुव अद दुकुम ?	mahuv a-adado kom ?
कृपया मुझे दो टिकट दें ।	please give me two tickets
मिन फादलक आ-अतिनि तथकिरतइन	min fadhlek ah-atini tathkirtain
मुझे पहले दर्जें के चार चाहिए ।	I want four first class
आ-अयिज अरबा-आ महल्लत दरजैला	ah-ayiz arba-ah mahallat darajaula
मैं, मरी पत्नी तथा तोंन बच्चे जो १६ साल से नीचें है ।	my wife and I and three children under 16
अना व ज़ौजती व थालाथीह अतफल दून अस्सादिसात अशार	anna wa zawjaty wa thalatheh atfal doon assadisat ashar
आपको पारिवारिक टिकट मिलेगा ।	you will get a family fare
साताहसाल अला ओजरात सफर आलिया	satahsal ala ojrat safar ailia
क्या आपके पास आज रात के लिए सीटें हैं ?	have you any seats for to-night ?
फीका-रा-सी लिल ले-लादी ?	feeka-ra-see lil lay-ladee ?

किराया क्या हैं ?	what is the charge ?
ग्रल उजरा काम ?	al ujrah kaam ?
यह लिस्ट (सूची) है ।	here is the list
हाथिही हिया ग्रल-ला-इहा	hathihi hia al-lah-iha
क्या टैक्स ग्रौर सेवा का खर्च शमिल है ?	are the tax and service charge included ?
इद-दारी बा विल खिद मा मा सू बीन ?	id-dah-ree bah wil khid mah mah soo been ?
ग्राप कितने प्रतिशत छूट देगे ?	what percentage do you discount ?
कम तहिसमू-न विल मिग्र ?	kam tahsimoon bil mia ?
कृपया मुझे कम से कम किराया बताईये (हवाई जहाज ग्रौर समुद्री जहाज से)	please let me know your least fares by air and sea
ग्रर्जु ग्रन तुग्रलिमूनी बिग्रदना उजूरिकम जव्वन व बहरन	arju an tolimooni bi adna ojoori kam javan wa baharan
उड़ान का नम्बर क्या है ?	what is the flight number ?
ताया रान निम-रा कम ?	tah yah rahn nim-rah kam ?
रवाना होने क्रा क्या समय है ?	what time is the departure ?
ऐय साहा मावहिद इसाफर ?	aya saha mawhid issafar ?
ग्राप किस बस से जाना चाहते हैं ?	by which bus do you want to go ?
फि ऐ बस्ता तोरीद ?	fi ai busta toureed ?
ग्राज कितने बजे नाव...(वहाँ) रवाना होगी	at what time does the boat leave for......to day ?
इम्ता ऍल-ब्राहबूर यीस्साहफ़ीर ईन्नाहर्द... ?	emta el-bahboor yessah feer ennahard ?

N

(वहाँ)... कौन सी बस जाती है ?	which bus goes to... ?
ओ तो बीस निम-रा कम बे-रूह ?	oh toh bees nim rah kam bay rooh ?
मैंने आपको कितना देना है ?	how much do I owe you ?
आ-विज़ काम	ah-wiz kam ?
कृपया मेरे लिए बिल ले आओ ।	please, bring the bill for me
मिन फ़ादलक (यिबलि) या	min fathlek (yibli) or atː il
अतनिल हिसाब	hisab
मैं आपको अच्छी यात्रा की दुआ देता हूँ	I wish you a good journey
महस सलमाह बिहिफ्ज-इल्लाह	mahas salamah bihifz-illah

Lesson 18

Travel By Bus
बस से सफर

क्या स्टेशन दूर हैं ?	is the station far ?
यात्रा अल-महात्ता बाहिदा ?	yatra al-mahatta bahida ?
मैं एक बस पास लेना चाहता हूँ ।	I would like to have a bus pass
ओरिद इश तिराक ओतोबिस	orid ishtirak otobis
कौन-सी बस दमिश्क जाती है ?	which bus goes to Damascus ?
अई बूस्ता तथहब इला अशहाम ?	ai busta tathhab ila asham ?
कण्डक्टर, मैं दो सीटें	conductor, I want to book
रिजर्व कराना चाहता हूँ	two seats
कौम-सारी, अाहरीद अन	kom-saree, ahreed an
आहलिज मकाहदिनी	ahliz makahdine
यह किस वक्त रवाना होती है ?	at what time does it leave ?
फ़ी अई वक़ितन तसीर ?	fi ai waqtin taseer ?
किराया कितना है ?	how much is the fare ?
बी-कम इत-ताज़ कारा ?	bee-kam it-tahz kahrah ?
वह कितनी दूर है ?	how much is the distance ?
चम मसाफ़ीआह या इशकाद बाहीद ?	cham masafe-ah or ishqad-ba heed ?
आप कहाँ बैठना पसन्द करेंगे	where would you like to·sit ?
एइन तोरीदोन अान ताजलिसो ?	ein toredon an tajliso ?

उधर कोने में	there in the the corner
हुनक फ़ि अज़ाविया	hunak fi azzavia
ठीक है, आप का समान कहाँ है ?	well, where is your luggage ?
हसनन ऐन अम्तिअतु-क	hasanan ein amtiatuk ?
मेहरबानी कर के समान नीचे ले जाइए	please take the luggale down
नज्ज़िलिल अफ़्श मिन फदलक	nazzil el afsh min fadlak
कृपया करके खिड़की खोल दे ।	please open the window
इफ्ता अश-शुब्बाक मिन फदलक	Iftah ash-shubbaak min fadlak
कंडकटर, थोड़ी देर ठहरो ।	conductor, wait for a while
मैं कुछ खाना चाहता हूँ	I want something to eat
कौम सारी श्रो- आह गाफ़ शवे	kom-sare, o-ah gaf
आरीद शैं लिल-अक़ल	shway areed shai lilaql
देर मत करो	don't be late
लाता आक-खीर	laata akh-khir
कृपा करके मुझे बताश्रो कि कहाँ पर उतरना है	please tell me where to get off
मिन फदलक, कल्ली अनजिल वीन	min fadlak, qullee anzil ween

Travel By Train
रेलगाड़ी से सफर

रेलवे स्टेशन कहाँ है ?	where is the railway station ?
अल महतता वीन ?	al-mahathah ween ?
कृपया बायी (दायी) तरफ मुड़ो ।	please turn to the left (right)
खुद यसारक (यामीनक) मिन फदलक	khud yasaarak (yomeenak) min fadlak

सीधा सामने	straight ahead
सीदी-ग्राह	seede-ah
क्या वहाँ के लिए कोई गाड़ी ?	Is there a train for ?
फी कितार ली ?	fee kitaar le ?
(वहाँ) के लिए पहली रेलगाड़ी किस	at what time does the first
वक़्त रवाना होती है ?	train leave for ?
मत्ता यक़ुमुल कितारूल अव्वल	mata yaqm-ul qitarul
इला ?	awal ila ?
किस प्लेटफार्म से गाड़ी जायेगी	from which platform does the
	train leave ?
इल आ त्रिही-ऊम मिन अन हूरा	el-ah tre-hi-oom min an-hoo-
सीफ ?	rah seef ?
टिकिट कहाँ खरीदे जा सकते है ?	where can the tickets be got ?
मिन ऐन, तुब्ता अत्त ज़ाकिर ?	min ein tobata attazaker ?
टिकिट घर में	at the booking office
मिन मक्रतब अत्ताजाकर	min maktab attazakar
मैं दो टिकटें रिजर्व कराना	I want to book two seats
चाहता हूँ ?	
आहरीद अन आहलिज मकाहदिनी	ahreed an ahliz makahdine
कृपया मुझे (वहाँ) तक का द्वितीय	give me second class ticket to?
श्रेणी का टिकिट दीजिए ।	a-atiny tath kara daraja
अ्रतिनी तथकारा दराजा थानिय	thania ila
इल!	
प्रतीक्षा-घर कहाँ है ?	where is the waiting room ?
ऐन क़ा-अतुल इन्तिज़ार	ein qa-a tul intizar ?

गाड़ी कब जायेगी ?	when does the train go ?
माता युसाफिरु-अल-क़ितार ?	mata yusafiru-al-qitar ?
जल्दी करो, वरना गाड़ो पकड़ने में देर हो जाएगी ।	hurry up or we shall be late for the train
अससरिअ व ला तअख्खरना अनिल क़ितार	assrih wa lla taakharna anal qitar
क्या यह सीट रिजर्व है ।	is this seat reserved ?
अल मकंद हादहा महज्जू	al-maqad haad haa mahjooz ?
स्लीपर कहाँ है ?	where is the sleeper ?
फायन आ-रा-बी यित इन-नोह्म ?	fayn ah-rah-bee yit innohm ?
क्या समान ठीक है ?	is the luggage all right ?
यत्रा-अल-आ अफश तमम ?	yatra-al-ah-afsh -tamam ?
गाड़ी सीटी बजा रही हैं ।	the train is whistling
अल क़ितार यासफिर	al qitar yasfir
तुम्हारी यात्रा शुभ हो	wish yon a good journey ?
महस सलमाह बिहिफज़-इल्लाह	mahas salamah bihifz-illah

Travel By Boat
नाव से सफर

समुद्र तट का छोटा रास्ता कौर-सा है ?	which is the shortest way to the beach ?
ऐता-री किन हो-आल एकूअसंर ईला अलबलाग ?	aita-rre kin hia-al aqusar ella alblage ?
क्या यह दूर (समीप) है ?	is it far (near)?
बाईद (करीब)	baeed (qareeb) ?

मुझे एक नाव चाहिए ।
श्राग़िज़ फुलुकाह

I want a boat
ayiz fulukah

नाव किस समय पहुँचेगी ?
इल-मार-किब्र हत-ऊप इमता ?

when does the boat arrive ?
el-mar-kib hat-oom
emtah ?

मेरे लिए दो सीटे रिजर्व कर दो ।
श्राहरीद श्रन श्राहलिज़ मकाहदिनी

I want to book two seats
ahreed an ahliz makahdine

श्राप कहाँ सफर करना चाहते हैं ?
इला एईन तीरोदीन श्रसफ़र हैं ?

where do you want to travel ?
illa ein toreeddon assafar ?

वहाँ (जगह का नाम)
इला

to
illa

मैं श्रापको कितना पैसा दूँ ?
इशग़ाद ताब्रि ?

how much do I pay you ?
ishgad tabbi ?

मेरा वीज़ा तैयार है ।
ताह शिरात श्रल-खुरुज जाहिज़ा

I have my visa ready
tah shirat al-khuruj jahiza

कैप्टन कहाँ है ?
फेयन इल-ग्रोब-तान ?

where is the captain?
fayn el-ohb-tahn ?

मौसम कैसा है ?
किफहल श्रताक़स ?

how is the weather ?
kifhal attaks ?

श्रच्छा है । मेरा ख्याल है, समुद्र
बेहतर है ।
श्रतावस जमील । श्रातक़िदु श्रन्नल
बह-र श्रफ़ज़ल

it is fine, I think the sea is
better
attaqus jameel ataqidu annal
bahr afjal

यह (नाव) कब तैयार हो जायेगी ?	when will it be ready ?
माता सातान ताहि मिन ताहादिरिहा ?	mata satantahi min tahdiriha?
दस मिनट में	in 10 minutes
फ़ि अशर दकाहिक	fi ashr dakahik
सीटें अच्छी है ।	the seats are good
इलमकानिक मुमतज़ा	ilmaqanik mumtaza
आओ हम चलें	come on, let us go
हया बिना	haya bina
यात्रा शुभ हो ।	bon voyage
माब्रा इस-साला-मा	maha-is -sa-la-ma

Lesson 19

In Town
शहर में

हम शहर देखना चाहते है ।	we want to see the town
नरीद नचुफ़िल मदीनीह	nareed nchufil madineh
यहाँ पर क्या-क्या दर्शनीय है ?	what is worth seeing here ?
फ़िशै जेन यिन्चफ ?	fi shay zain yinchaf ?
प्रतिदिन का क्या किराया है ?	what is the charge per day ?
बी काम इल-योम	bee kam el-yowm
टैक्सी से	by taxi
फ़िल-तिक्सी	fil tixi
प्राइवेट कार से	by private car
फ़िल खसूसी सियारा	fil khasusi siyara
बस से	by bus
फ़िल बस्त	fil bast
एक यात्रा का कितना खर्चा है ?	what is the charge for a trip
बी-काम इर-रिह्-ला	bee-kam ir-reh-la
मैं किराये पर कहाँ से ले सकता हूँ	where can I hire···?
ग्रा-दार ग्रा-ऊग गार फायन ?	ah-dahr ah-ug gar fayn ?
एक कार (टैक्सी)	a car (taxi)
सियारा (तिक्सी)	siyara (tixi)

वहाँ जाने प्रोर वापिस श्राने में कितना समय लगेगा ?	how long will it take to go there and get back ?
चम याखीथ बक़्त मिन हनी इला-हनक	cham yakhith waqt min hnee ila hnak ?
किस प्रकार एक व्यक्ति जा सकता है ?	how can one go to ?
इज़ जी इल-वा हिद यि-रुह ?	iz-zi il-wah hid yi-rooh ?
प्रजायव घर को इलाल-मत-ग्राह हाफ़िल बतनी	to national museum ilal mat ah hafll watani
चिड़िया घर गिने नित इल हा यां-वा-नत	the zoo ge nay nit il ha ya-wa-naʈ
पार्क इला गिनना	the park il-ge-nay-nah
पुस्तकालय इल मक ता-बा	the library il-mak-ta-ba
हमें ऐतिहासिक स्थान पर ने चलो	take us to some places of historical interest
इखियनी ग्राह नतिफार्‌राज ग्रलाल मा-हल्लातिल ग्रथारीयीह	ikhithne-ah ntifarraj alal ma-hall atil athariyeh
कृपया मुझे कोई दिलचस्प स्थय दिखाएं ।	please show me the sights of interest
मिन फ़ादलक वार-री-नी इल-ग्रा मा किन इल मू हिम मा ।	min fadlak wahr-ree-nee il-a-ma-kin il-moo him mah

हमें अजायबघर ले चलो ।	take us to the national museum
इखिथिनी-ग्राह इलाल-मत ग्राह	ikhithne-ah ilal-mat-ah
हाफ़िल वतनी	hafil watni
अजायनघर कब बन्द होता है ?	when does the museum close ?
इमता इल मत हूफ़ यि-फिल्ल ?	imta il mat huff yi-fill ?
क्या यह रास्ता अन्दर जाने का है ?	is this the way to the entrance ?
ही या दी सिक-कित ?	hee yah dee sik-kit ?
मुझे एक नक्शा च हिए	I want a map
ओरिद खरीता	orid kharita
क्या तुम्हारे पास कोई नक्शा है ?	have you any map ?
हइ इनदैक खरीता ?	haei indaek kharita ?
यह कितने का है ?	how much is it ?
बकैम ?	bikaem ?
अन्दर जाने की क्या टिकिट है ?	what is the admission fee ?
बी-काम इद दो-खूल	bee-kam id doh-khool ?
अगर हमारे पास समय हुआ तो हम फाईन आर्ट गैलरी देखने जाएंगे ।	If we have time, we shall visit the fine arts gallery
लोव-मे आ-ना वात हुन-रूह मत-हूफ़ एलफो नन इल गा-मी ला	low-may ah-nah-waht hun-rooh-mat-huff elfoh nun el ga-mee-la
मुख्य गिरजाघर	the cathedral
एलका तिद-रा लीया	elka tid-rah leeya
चत्रकला	paintings
र रासमि	ir rasme

यह वाकई ग्रच्छी है ।

his is really good

ह्राया जयिद बिल हाकीका

hatha jaid bil haqiqa

हुमारी हार्दिक इच्छा है कि हम ग्रपने देश (भारत) जाने से पहले सब कुछ देख लें ।

our intention is to see every thing before we go back to India

कसदुना नशुफ़ कुल शै क़ाबल मा नारजाह इला बिलादिल ग्रल हिंद ।

qasduna nashuf kul shai qabl ma narjah ila biladil al hind

Lesson 20

Shopping
खरीददारी

सबसे नजदीक बाजार कहाँ है ?	where is the nearest bazaar ?
ऐयनॆ अ्करब बज़ार ?	aeynae akrab bazar ?
मुझॆ वह (वस्तु)···कहाँ मिल सकती है ?	where can I get ··· ?
अह-अहास्सील···?	ah-ahassel ·· ?
मैं···खरीदना चाहता हूं	I want to buy···
अह-आरीद आह-अशतिरि	ah-areed ah-ashtri ···
मैं सूती कपड़ा खरीदना चाहता हूँ	I want to buy cotton cloth
आह-आरीद आह-अशतिरि फ़ोस्तान कतिन	ah areed ah-ashtiri fostan qitin
मैं एक रेशमी कमीज चाहता हूँ ।	I want a silk shirt
उरीदु कमी-स हरीर	oreedu kameece hareer
आप कौन-सा रंग चाहते हैं ?	what colour do you want ?
अय्यु लौनिन तुरीदु ?	ayu launin tureedu ?
मैं सदा हल्के भूरे कपड़ों को पसन्द करता हूँ ।	I always prefer light-brown clothes
अन्ना अफ़ाद्दिल दाग्र इमान मला-बिस बनॆ फातीह	anna afaddil daa imaan mala-abis bunee faatch

इस कपड़े में आपके पास कौन-कौन से रंग हैं ?	what colour do you have in this cloth ?
शाहल अलवान हाली इन्दक मिन हल (क़िमिश) या ख़लाक़ ?	shahal alwan halee indak min hal (kimish) or khalaq ?
क्या तुम्हारे पास कुछ अच्छा है ? फी अन-दक़ हा-गा आ-सन ?	have you something better ? fee an-dak ha-ga ah-san ?
यह प्रति मीटर कितने का है ? वी-क़ाम दी इल मितरि ?	how much is it per metre ? bee-kam dee ill mitri ?
यह काफी महँगा है । दा राली अवी	it is too expensive da ralee awee
मुझे कुछ सस्ता दिखाओ आह-आरीद शैं अरखास	I want something cheaper ah-areed shay arkhas
यह अच्छी कमीज है । इन्नहू क़मीसुन जमील	It is a nice shirt innaho kameesun jameel
मुझे कोई दूसरा रंग चाहिए । उरीदु लौनिन आखर	I want another colour oreedu lawnan akhar
क्या यह सिकुड़ेगा ? दी बित किश ?	will it shrink ? dee bit kish ?
मुझे जुराबों के तीन जोड़े चाहिएँ । उरीदु थलाथत अज़वाज जवारिब	I want three pairs of socks oreedu thalathat azwaj jawareb
मुझे कुछ बड़े साईज का दिखाओ ।	show me something of larger size
वार-री ना हा-गा मा-अस किबीर	wahr-reena ha-ga ma-as kibee
यह सचमुच अच्छी है । हाथा जय्यिद बिल हक़ीक़	this is really good hathh jaid bil haqiqa

कृपया मुझे बिल दे दो ।

please give me the bill

मिन फादलक इद-दी-नी ब्र-सीमा

min fahdluk id-dee-nee a-seema

मैं पैसे कहाँ दूं ?

where do I pay ?

अद-फा फेयन ?

ad-fah fayn ?

कृपया मुझे रसीद दे दो ।

please give me receipt

मिन फादलक इद-दी-नी वासलि

min fahdluk id-dee-nee wahsli

कृपया इसे बांध दे ।

please wrap it

मिन फ़ादलीक लिफ़नी-याह (यदि

min fadhlek liflee-yaha (if

कारक पुल्लिग हो) (लिफ़ली याहा-
यदि कारक स्त्रीलिंग हो)

object is m.) (liflee-yaha-if
object is f.)

कृपया मुझे दे दे ।

please give me

मिन फ़ादलीक ब्राह-ब्रतनी

min fahdlek ah-atni

कृपया इन्हें ˜होटल भिजवा दें ।

please send these things to
the hotel··· ··

मिन फ़ादलीक इरसिल्ली हल
ब्राशया-ब्राह इलाल होटेल···

min fadhlek ircilli hal ashya-
ah ilal hotail····

Lesson 21

On the Phone
टेलिफोन पर

क्या मैं आपका टेलीफोन इस्तेमाल कर सकता हूँ ?	may I use your telephone please ?
अकदर असता मिल तिलिफूनक मिन फदलक ?	Aqdar asta mil tileefoonak min fadlak ?
क्या आपके पास टेलीफोन डायरैक्टरी है ?	do you have a telephone directory ?
हैल इनदैक दैलिल तिलिफ़ोनेत ?	hael indaek daelil tilifonaet ?
टेलीफोन खराब है । इत तिलीफून अतलान	the telephone is out of order it tileefoon atlaan
लाईन रूकी हुई है अल-खत मशगूल	the line is busy al-khat mashghool
क्या मैं श्री रमन पाल से बात कर सकता हूँ ?	could I speak to Mr. Raman Pal ?
मुमकिन अकल्लिम अस-सय्यिद रमन पाल ?	mumkin akallim as-sayyid Raman Pal ?
माफ़ करना नम्बर ग़लत है । आसिफ़ रकम ग़लत	sorry, wrong number aasif rakam ghalat
वह यहाँ नहीं है। हुव्वा मुश मावजूद	he is not here huwwa mush mawjood

कौन बोल रहा है	who is speaking ?
मीन यिताकाल्लम ?	meen yetakallam ?
यह अशोक बोल रहा है	this is Ashok speaking
अना अशोक	anna Ashok
मैं···(जगह का नाम)···से बोल रहा हूँ	I am talking to you from...
अतकल्लमु मुअक मिनल······	atakalamu muka minal
क्या तुम फुरसत में हो ?	are you free ?
मा-आह इन्दक शै या फ़रगान ?	ma-ah indak shay **or** fargham ?
क्यों ?	why ?
लिमाज़ा ?	limaza ?
मैंने तुम्हें लम्बे समय से नहीं देखा है ।	I haven't seen you for a long time
लम अरा-क मुनज मुद्दतिन तवीलतन	lam arak munaz mudatin twee latan
मैं यह चाहता हूँ कि तुम शाम मेरे साथ बाहर गुज़ारो	I want you to spend the evening out with me
उरीदु-क अन तसहर मई	oreedu-ka an tashar mai
तुम अपना काम कब खत्म करोगे ?	what time would you finish your work ?
फ़ि ऐहार साहत तोन्हीं अमालक ?	fi aihar sahat tonhee amalak?
दो बजे	at 2 o'clock
अस-सा अतुस् सानिय	assa atus saniah
ठीक है, मैं तुम्हारे पास आ जाऊंगा	alright I will be with you
तय्यिब सग्रकूनु मअक	taib saakounu maak

कब ?	when ?
मता ?	mata ?
ढाई बजे	at 2.30
अस्सा अतुस्सानिय वन्निस्फु	assa atus saniah wanisfu
तब तक के लिए इजाज़त	so long
इल्लिक़ा	ila alliqa
खुदा हाफ़िज़	good-bye
बिखानिरक	bikha tirak
मैं आपको कितने ग़ैसे दूं ?	how much do I pay you ?
इशग़ाद ताबि ?	Ishgad tabbi ?

Operator
ओपरेटर

सुबह की नमस्ते, ओपरेटर मुभे कुवेंत 569808 नम्बर चाहिए	good morning, operator, I want Kuwait 569808
सबा ग्रैल खैर, अमिल इत-तिलीफ़ून ओरिद ग्रैल कुवैत 569808	sabah ael kher, aamil it-tilee-fon orid ael Kuwait 569808
मैं पर्सनल (निजी) कॉल करना चाहता हूँ	I want to make a personal call
ओरिद मोकैलमैं शख़सिय्यैं	orid mokaelmae shakhsiyyae
माफ़ करना, लाईन रुकी हुई है	sorry, the line is busy
आसिफ, अल-ख़त मशग़ूल	aasif, al-khatt mashghool
हैलो यह रमन पाल बोल रहा हैं	hello, this is Raman Pal speaking
ग्रैलो ग्रैने रमन पाल	helo aenae Raman Pal

क्या मैं सीधा फोन कर सकता हूँ ?	can I dial direct ?
हैल युगैद खत्त मोबेशिर ?	hael yugaed khatt mobaes hir ?
कृपया और धीरे बोलो	please speak more slowly
मिन फादलक इत-काल-लिम आला-मा-लक	min fahdluk it-kal-lim ahlah-mah-lak
कृपया इसे दोहराओ	repeat it, please
बित-ऊल ए मिन फादलक	bit-ool ay min fahdluk
मैं एकस्टैंनशन चाहता हूँ	I want extension
ओरिद ऐल दैलखिलि रकम	orid ael daelkhili rakam
वह कब वापिस आयेंगे ?	when will he be back ?
मैते येरगा ? (तेरगा-स्त्रीलिंग)	maetae yaergaa? (taergaa-f)
आप के लिए एक टेलीफोन सूचना है ।	there is a telephone message for you
फ़ी रिसाला तालाफूनिया लाक	fee risala talafooniya lak
क्या आप उसे कह सकते है मैंने बुलाया है ?	will you tell him I called ?
मिन फदलक कोल लैंहो इन्ही इत्तसलत ? (लैंहे-स्त्रीलिंग)	min fadlak kol laeho innee ittasalt ? (laehae-f)
क्या आप समझ गये हैं ।	do you understand ?
ऐन्ता फा-हिम ?	enta fah-him ?
आपका क्या नाम है ?	what is your name ?
इस्समुक ऐ ?	Isasmuk ay ?
मेरा नाम रमन पाल है	my name is Raman Pal
इसमि रमन पाल	ismi Raman Pal

उस काल का क्या मूल्य था ?

what was the cost of that call ?

बिकैं हेजिहि ग्रैल मोकैलमैं ?

bikae haezihi ael mokael mae?

इसकी रसीद मुझे दे दें
श्राहतिनि बिहि वसल

give me a receipt for it
ah-tini bihi wasl

Lesson 22

At a draper's shop
कपड़े की दुकान पर

कोई सेवा जनाब ?	any service, sir ?
अ यात खिदमा या सईदी ?	ayat khidma ya saidi ?
मैं कुछ कपड़ा खरीदना चाहता हूँ उरीदु अन अश्तरी किमाशन	I want to buy some cloth oreedu an ashtari kimashan
आप कैसा कपड़ा चाहते हैं ?	what sort of cloth do you want ?
मन नौह अलक़िमाश अल्लाथि तोरीदोह ?	man nowh alqimash allathi toredoh ?
आप को किस लिए चाहिए ? लिमा ज़ा तुरीदोह ?	what do you want it for ? lima za torredoh ?
मैं सूती कपड़ा खरीदना चाहता हूँ आह-आरीद आह-अश्तिरि फ़ोस्तान क़ितिन	I what to buy a cotton dress ah-areed ah-ashtiri fostan qitin
मैं सूट के लिए लेना चाहता हूँ उरीदु मिन अज्लि बदला	I want it for a suit oreedu min ajl badla
मैं ऊंची किस्म का ऊनी कपड़ा चाहता हूँ श्रोरीदोहो जोखन मिन आह-ख़ा-सिफ	I want woollen of superior quality oreedoho joukhan min ah-la sinf

यह (बुरा) (अच्छा) है ।
this is (bad) (good)

हाथी-आह (मोब जेन) (जेन)
hathi-ah (mob zain) (zain)

यह रंग नहीं ठहरेगा
the colour won't stand

हाथल्लौन ला यदूम
hatha alloun la yadoom

मैं यह नहीं चाहता
I don't want it

मा-आह-बीख
ma-ah-bekh

मैं आपको एक और टुकड़ा दिखाऊंगा
I will show you another piece

सउरी कंकित्अतन उखरा
sa-orika qitatan okhra

मुझे यकीन हैं आप इसे ले लेंगे
I am sure you will take it

आना मुताह अकिद अन्नाहो सय्योंज
ana mutah akid annaho

बोकोम
sayoji bokom

यह बहुत नर्म है ।
this is very soft

हाथिहि नाहिमा जिद्दन
hathihi nahima jiddan

इसमें आपके पास कौन-कौन से
what colours do you

रंग है ?
have in this material ?

शःहल अलवन हाली इन्दक मिन
sahal alwan halee indak

हाल (क्रिमिश) या खलाक ?
min hal (qimash) or

khalaq ?

यह कितने का है ?
how much is it ?

बिकेम ?
bi kaem ?

प्रति मीटर ?
per metre ?

इल मिन रि ?
ill mitri ?

यह बहुत मंहगा है ।
this is too expensive

हाथी-आह गालि बायाद
hathe ah- ghali wayed

क्या आपके पास कुछ सस्ता है ?	have you something cheape
फी अन-दक हागा आर-खस ?	fee an-dak haga ahrkhas ?
इसमें एक छेद है ।	there is a hole in this
यूगैंद सोकब फि है जें ।	yugaed sokb fi haezae
आप के पास जो सबसे अच्छा है वही मुझे दिखाईए ।	show me the best you have
अरिनी अफ़दल मा इन्दक	arini afdhal ma indak
यह अच्छी किसम (क्वालिटी) का है ।	it is of better quality
इन्न हा मिन सिन्फिन अफ़दल ।	innaha min sinfin afdhal
मैं यह वाला लूंगा ।	I will take this one
आकुद हादि	a kuda hadhi
क्या आप मेरा नाप लोगे ?	could you measure me ?
हैल योमकिन ग्रेन तकिस लि ?	hael yom kin aen takis li ?
कृपया मुझे चार मीटर काट दीजिए ।	cut me 4 metres please
इक्तग्र ..ी अर्बंग्रत अम्तार मिन फदलिक	iqtah li arbaat amtar min fadhlik
मैं आपको कितना पैसा दूँ	how much do I pay you ?
इशग़ाद ताबि ?	ishgad tabbi ?
मुझे इसकी रसीद दे दो ।	give me a receipt for it
आहतिनि बिहि वसल	ah-tini bihi wasl
बिल में गलती है ।	there is a mistake in the bill
फी रूल-ता-फिल हि-साब	fee rul-tah-fill hi-sab

Lesson 23

Laundry and dry-cleaning

धुलाईघर और
ड्राई-क्लीनिंग

क्या यहाँ पर ड्राई-क्लीनिंग की सेवाएँ is there a dry-cleaning service
प्राप्त हो सकती हैं । | around here ?
फी-हिना तन-तूर-ले श्रो-री-यिब ? | fee hina tan-toor-lay oh-ree-yib ?

यह कमीज़ धोने के लिए है । | this shirt is for washing
इल श्रा मीस दा लिल्रह सील । | elah mess da lil rah seel

इसको गर्म पानी में मत धोना । | don't wash this in hot water
मा-तिर-सिलशि दी फी मी-या सोखना | ma-tir-silshi dee fee mi-yah sokhnah

कालर को कड़ा कर दो | starch the collar
नाश-शी इल-याश्रा | nash-shee el-yaah

क्या आप इस बटन को सी | can you sew this button ?
सकते हैं ?
तिदार तिरक्-किब इज़-जू | tidahr tirak-kib iz-zoo rahr
रार दा ? | da ?

मैं इस सूट को साफ और इस्तरी करबाना चाहता हूँ ।

I want this suit to be cleaned and ironed

अना आ-विज इल-बाद-ला दी तित-रि-सिल वि तित-कि-वी ।

anah ah-wiz el-bad·la dee tit-ri-sil wi tit ke·wee

इसको गुनगुने और ठंडे पानी से मत धोना ।

don't wash this in lekewarm and cold water

मा-तिर-सिलीश दी फी माया फ़ातिर व बारदा ।

matir-silshi dee fi mi·yah fatir wa barda

माँड (स्टार्च) मत लगाना ।

do not starch

बा-लाशनि-शा

ba-lashni-sha

क्या आप यह धब्बा मिटा सकते हैं ?

can you remove this stain ?

ति-दार ति-ताल-ला इल बी आ दी ?

ti-dahr ti-tal-lah el- bo ah dee ?

पॉकिट फटी हुई है ।

the pocket is torn

इल-गायब मख रू ।

el-gayb makh-roo

क्या आप इसे ठीक कर सकते है ?

can you mend this ?

ओरिद रैफित हेज़े मिन फदलक ?

orid raeffit haezae min fadlak ?

कल सुबह कपड़ों को इस्तरी कर देना

iron the clothes tomorrow morning

ईको वाचिर इस्सुब

ekow bachir issubh

यह मेरी नहीं है ।

this is not mine

हेज़ै लैयसै मिलक्कि

haezae laeysae milki

यह कब तक तैयार हो सकता है ?

when will it be ready ?

मैते ते तेकुन गेहिज़े ।

maetae tae tackun gaehizae

यह जरूरी है ।	this is necessary
हांदि दरूरियाह ।	hadi drurieyah
मुझे आज इसकी जरूरत हैं ।	I need it today
ओरिदओऐ ऍल योम ।	oridohae ael yom
एक कपड़ा इसमें से गुम है ।	there's one piece missing
नकिस किता आ ।	nakis kita-a
मैंने आपको कितना देना है ।	how much do I pay you ?
इशग्राद ताबि ?	ishagad tabbi ?

Lesson 24

At the Barber's shop & Beauty saloon
नाई की दुकान और सौन्दर्य सैलून

क्या आप बाल कटवाना चाहते हैं ?	do you want to have your hair cut, sir ?
ा-तुरीदु अन अकॉस शारका या सय्यिदी ?	a-torredu an aqoss sharaka ya saidi ?
या आप शेव बनाना चाहते हैं, नाब ?	do you want to shave, sir ?
ा-तुरीदु अन तहिलक़ या सय्यिदी ?	a-torredu an tahleq ya saidi ?
ृपया मैं बाल कटबाना चाहता हूँ	I want a haircut, please
तोरिद अस इल शार मिन फादलक	orid ass il shaar min fadlak
् शेब करवाना चाहता हूँ ।	I want to have a shave
ाह-आरीद आह-आहलीक या लहयीती	ah-areed ah-ahlek or lihyeti
् पहले बाल बनवाना और फिर व करवाना चाहता हूँ ।	I want to have my hair cut first, and then shave
रीदु अन अक़ुस स शअ्री सुम·म हलुक़ जब्नी	oreedu an aqossa shari sum— mum ahlog zaqni
हुत लम्बे नहीं	not too long
ा रखालिली-शा-आहरं तिवील	la-tkha lilee-sha-ahar tiweel

बहुत अधिक मत काटना	don't cut too much
मुत ओस सिश कि तीर	mut os sis ki teer
बहुत छोटे नहीं	not too short
लात क़ासिर इशा आहर	lat-quyssir isha-ahar
किनागें से और काट दो ।	cut more off the sides
कुस अक्तार दर मदार इर-रस	qus akthar dar madar ir-ras
कृपया ऊपर से मत काटो ।	don't cut any off the top plea
खुफ फिफ़ इलआ फ़ाबिल गा-वा न	khuf-fif ela fawil-ga-wa n
निब बास मिन फादलुक	bass min fahdluk
इसको बहुत छोटा मत करो	don't cut it too short
लै तांओमो कासिरान गिदेन	lae ta-osso kasiran gideaen
मैं बालों को कटवाना चाहता हूँ (तरफ से)	I part my hair (on the side)
अना बाफ़रि शाह-री (आला इल-गानब)	anah bafri shah-ree (ahlah i ganb)
कुछ अधिक··· (इस तरफ से)	a little more off the···
कसर अकतार मिन	kassar aktar min···
गर्दन	neck
ऐल ख़ेल्फ़	ael khaelf
तरफ़े	sides
ऐल गैवेनिब	ael gaewaenib
क्या आप कृपया मेरी (दाढ़ी) (मूंछे) ठीक कर देंगे ।	would you please trim n (beard), (moustache) ?
ओरित तवदिब ऐन (जैहन) (नैनैव) मिन फदनक ?	orid tawlib ael (zaekt (shaenaebb) min fadhlak ?

कृपया, कैंची से केवल	scissors only, please
ग्रैल मैंग्रस फ़कत मिन फदलक	ael maeass fakatt min fadlak
सौन्दर्य सैलून	beauty saloon
सलोनी ताजमिल	salone tajmil
मैं अपने बाल सैंट करवाना चाहता हूँ	I want my hair set
ग्रा-ग्रारीद शा-ग्राहर्रासि	ah-areed sha-aharrasi
कृपया ऊपर को कंघी कीजिए ।	please comb it upwards
आयोऊ अन तोमशित ग्रोहो इला फोग कोउग ।	ayou an tomashit oho ila foug
मैं अपने बालों को रंगवाना चाहता हूँ	I want my hair tinted
ग्राह-ग्रारीद ग्राहा-असबाग़ शा-ग्राहरि	ah-areed aha-asbagh sha-ahri
(हल्का रंग) (उसी रंग के)	(a lighter colour) (the same colour)
(लोनी अफ़्ताह) (नाफ़सिल्लोनी)	(lone aftah) (nafsillone)
मुझे कितनी देर इन्तज़ार करनी पड़ेगी	how long must I wait ?
इश-ग्राह-कद लाज़ीम ग्रो-ग्राह-गाफ़ ?	ish-ah-qad lazem o-ah-gaf ?
मैं स्थायी लहर चाहता हूँ ।	I want a permanent wave
ग्राह-ग्रारीद अक्वी शाग्राहरी	ah-areed akwi sha-ah-ri
क्या मैं मिलने का समय इसके लिए तय कर सकता हूँ	can I make an appointment for···
ग्रा-दार अखुद मे-अदग्रा-ला शन···	ah-dahr akhud may-adah-lah shan···
मैं अपने बाल धुलवाना चाहता हूँ	I want my hair washed
ग्राह-ग्रारीद ग्राह-ग्रगसील शा-ग्राहर रसि	ah-areed ah-aghsel sha-ahar rasi

(शैंम्पू) (तेल मालिश)	(shampoo) (massage)
(शाम्पू) मसाज	(shampoo) (massage)
मुझे किसी भी तेल की जरूरत नहीं है	I don't want any oil
ले ओरिद जित	lae orid zet
मैं नाखूनों और हाथों की सुन्दरता बढ़ाना चाहता हूँ ।	I want a manicure
आ-आरीद इम-आ-अदिल अदाफिर	ah-areed im-ah-adail adhafir
धन्यवाद	thank you
शुक्रन	shokran
मैं आपको कितना देना है ?	how much do I owe ?
कैम ऐल हिसेब	kame ael hisaeb

Lesson 25

Stationery, Book Shop
लेखन सामग्री तथा
किताबों की दुकान पर

सबसे नजदीक (किताबों) (लेखन सामग्री) की दुकान कहाँ है ?	where is the nearest (book shop) (stationery shop) ?
ऐयने अकरब (मैकैबे) (मैकतैबे)	aeynae akrab (maekaebae) (maektaebae) ?
कोई सेवा जनाब '	any service, sir ?
अयात खिदमा	ayat khidma ?
यहाँ कौन सी पुस्तकें बिकती हैं ?	what books are sold here
मा हियल कुतुब अल्लती तुबाग्र हुना	ma hial kutub alalti tubah huna ?
यह लिस्ट है, जनाब	here is the catalogue, sir
तफाद दुल अल फ्रेहरिस्त या सय्यिदी	tafad dul al fahrisst ya saidi
इस लिस्ट में आपको बहुत सी अलग-अलग किताबें मिलेंगी ।	in this catalogue you find many different books
फ़ी हाजल फ़ेहरिस्त ताजिद इद-त कुतुब मु-तनव्विग्र	fi hajal fahrisst tajid iddat kutub motanawia
मैं एक पुस्तक खरीदना चाहता हूँ ।	I want to buy a book
ओरिद शिरा कितेब	orid shira kitaeb

क्या तुम्हारे पास कोई अंग्रेजी-अरबी जेबी डिक्शनरी है ?	have you any English-Arabic pocket dictionary
हैइ इनदैक इनगिलिजि-अरबी लिल गिब ?	haci indaek ingilizi-arabi kamous lil gib
मुझे एक अंग्रेजी-अरबी की डिक्शनरी चाहिए ।	I want an English-Arabic dictionary.
उरीदु क़ामूस इन्गिलिजि अरबी	oreedu kamous ingilizir arabi
यह अच्छी नहीं है ।	this is not good
हाथीय मोब जेनीह	hathey mob zaineh
आप किस क़िस्म का चाहते हैं ?	what kind do you want ?
अय्यु नौअ तुरीद	aiu nauh toreed ?
मुझे सबसे अच्छी किस्म का चाहिए।	I want the best quality
अरीदु मिन अहसीन सिन्फ़	oreedu min ahsani sinf
आपको यह कैसी लगी ?	how do you like this one ?
कैईफ़ ताजिद हाथा ?	kai-eef tajid hatha?
शायद आपको यह पसन्द आयेगी ।	you may like it
रूब्बामा तुहिम्बुल	rubbama tuhibbul
हाँ, यह अच्छी है ।	yes this is good
ना-अह-आम हाथीय जेनीह	na-ah-am, hathey zaineh
मुझे यकीन है आप इस ले लेंगे ।	I am sure you will take it
आना मुताह अकिद अन्नाहो सय्योजि बोकोम	ana mutah akid annaho sayoji bokom
इसकी क्या किमत होगी ?	what will it cost ?
ख़ाम तकील ?	cham takeel ?

यह बहुत ज्यादा है	this is too much
हाथा काथीरों जिददन	hatha katheero jaiddan,
क्या आपके पास कोई श्रंग्रेजी मैग्जीन है ?	have you any English magazine ?
हल इन्दाकुम जल्लातुन इंक्लीज़ीय ?	hal indakom jallatun inglizieh
बया आपके पास दुनिया का नक्शा है ?	have you a map of the world?
हल इन्दाकुम खरीततन लिल आलम ?	hal indakom kharetatan lil alam ?
मैं एक सड़क का नक्शा खरीदना चाहता हूँ	I want to buy a road map
श्रोरिद शिरा खरीता लिल तोरोक ।	orid shira kharita lil torok
क्या आपके पास शहर का नक्शा है ?	do you have a map of the city
व हल इन्दाकुम खरीता लिल मदीना ?	wa hal indakom kharita lil madina ?
नक्शे की क्या कीमत है ?	what is the price of the map ?
कम समनुल खरीता	kam samnul kharita ?
क्या आपके पास कोई ताश है ?	do you have any playing cards ?
हैई इनदैक वरक लीब ?	hae indaek waark leeb ?

मैं एक (पेन) (पेंसिल) (बाल पेन) खरीदना चांहता हूँ	I want to buy a (pen) (pencil) (ball point pen)
प्रोरिद शिरा (कलम हिब्र) (कलम रोसास) (कलम हिबू गेफ)	orid shira (kalam hibr) (kalam rosas) (kalam hibr gaef)
मुझे पत्र लिखने के लिए कुछ कागज चाहिए	I want some letter-paper
उरीदु औरा-क़ मकातीब	oreedu auraqa makateeb
मुझे कुछ लिफ़ाफ़े भी चाहिएँ	I also want some envelopes
उरीदु ऐज़न बझ्ज़ल मुग़लफ़ात	oreedu aizan bazal moghalfat
बड़े साईज़ के	of larger size
मा अस कि-बीर	maas kibeer
कृपया मुझे दें	please give me
मिन फ़ादलीक आह्-अतनी	min fadhlek ah-atni
(लिखने वाला पैंड) (रखाचित्र बनाने वाला कागज)	(writing pad) (drawing paper)
(बलॉक वरक) (वरक रैसम)	(blok warak) (warak raesm)
कृपया मुझे रसीद दे दें ,	please give me a receipt
मिन फादलीक इद-दी-नी वासलि	min fadlek id dee nee wasli
मैं आपको कितना (पैसा) हूँ	how much do I pay you ?
इशगाद ताबि ?	ishgad tabbi ?

Lesson 26

At the cinema, Theatre
सिनेमा-थियेटर में

मैं पिक्चर (सिनेमा) देखना चाहता हूँ आह-आरीद आह-आरूह इस-सिनीमा।	I want to go to the cinema ah-areed ah-aruh iss cinema
क्या तुम मुझे कोई अच्छी फिल्म बता सकते हो ? हेल तेनसानि बि फिल्म गोय्यिद ?	can you recommend me a good film hael taensahani bi film goeyyid ?
ड्रामा (सुखद नाटक) दरामा (कोमिदये)	drama (comedy) drama (komidyae)
आज रात को स्थानीय पिक्चर हाल में कौन सी पिक्चर चल रही है शिनहिल अफ़लान बिस-सिनीमा इल्लायला ?	what film is at the local cinema hall tonight ? shinhil aflan bis-cinema illayla ?
कितने बजे शुरू होती है ? मेतै येबदे ?	what time does it begin ? maetae yaebdae ?
थियेटर कहाँ है ? अल-मसरा वीन ?	where is the theatre ? al-masrah ween?
बालकोनी सीट की क्या कीमत है ?	how much price is a balcony seat ?
बी-काम कार-सी वाला कोन ?	bee-kam kar-see bala kohn ?

कम से कम कितने पैसे है ?
बी-काम आर-खस ताज-काह-रा ?

what is the minimum charge ?
bee-kam ahr-khas tahz-kah-rah ?

क्या आपके पास आज रात के लिए कुछ सीटें है ?
फी-का-रा-सी लिल ले-ला-दी ?

have you any seats for tonight ?
fee ka-ra-see lil-lay-la-dee ?

कृपया मुझे दो टिकटें दे दें ।
मिन फ़दलीक आहातिनि ताथकीर ताईन

please give me two tickets
min fadhlek ah-atini tathkir tain

यह सीटें कहाँ है ?
वेनिल महाल्लात ?

where are these seats ?
wav-nil mahallat ?

बाक्स में
फ़िल लोगी

in a box
fil loge

कोने में
फ़िल अखीर

in the rear
fil-akher

क्या ये बीच में है ?
हलिल महाल्लात फ़िन-नुस ?

are they in the centre ?
halil mahallat fin-nus ?

कितने बजे शो खत्म होता है ?
मेतैं येनतेहि एल आरद ?

what time does the show end ?
maetae yaentaehi ael ard ?

क्या यह सीटें अच्छी हैं ?
इल महल्लत ज़ाइनीह ?

are these good seats ?
il mahallat zaineh ?

मध्यावकाश कितनी देर का है ?
इल-इस-तिराहा अद-दी-ए ?

how long is the interval ?
el-is tiraha ad-dee-ay ?

कौन नाच (गा) रहा है ?	who is dancing (singing) ?
मेन येरकोस (योगेनि) ?	maen yaerkos (yogaenni) ?
यह अच्छी (बुरी) फ़िल्म है ।	this is a good (bad) film
हाथीय जेनीह (हाथीय मोब जेनीह) फ़िल्म ।	hathey zaineh (hathey mob zaineh) film
मैं मध्यावकाश के बाद घर जाना चाहता हूँ ।	I want to go home after the interval
अन्ना उरीद अरुह इला अल-बयत बा दल इसनिराहह	anna ureed arooh elaa al-bayt ba dal isnirahah

Lesson 27

At the night club
नाईट-क्लब में

क्या तुम किसी अच्छे नाइट-क्लब के बारे में सुझाव दे सकते हो ?	can you recommend a good night club ?
हैल तनसानि बी मैलहे लैयलि गैय्यिद	hael tansani bi maelhae laeyli gaeyyid ?
हमें किसी अच्छे नाईट क्लब में ले चलो	take us to a good night club
इखिथनी-आह इला माल्ही-आह जेन	ikhithne-ah ila malhe-ah zain
क्या शाम की पोशाक आवश्य हैं ?	is evening dress necessary ?
हैल लिब्स ऐल साहरा-दारुरि ?	hael libs ael sahra daruri ?
आपका स्वागत है	you are welcome
अहलान वा सहलान	ahlan wa sahlan
मैं चार व्यक्तियों की एक मेज चाहता हूँ	I want a table for four persons
आह-आरीद तवलीह हक अरबा-आहा	ah-areed tawleh hak arba-ah a
आप कहाँ बैठना पसन्द करेंगे ?	where do you like to sit ?
एइन तोरोदोन आन ताजलिसो ?	in toredon an tasliso ?
कोने में	in the corner
फिर रोक-नि	fir tchk-ni

क्या यहाँ पर सेवा का खर्चा भी लिया जाता है ?	is there a service charge ?
हाल फ़ि मसारिफ ?	hal fi masarif ?
क्या वहाँ पर आज फ्लोर शो है ?	is there a floor show today ?
हैल यूगैद आरद फैनि अल-यौम ?	hael yugaed ard faeni al-youm ?
कृपया मुझे शराब की लिस्ट दीजिए	please give me the wine list
आह-आतनिल-मिन लिसटिल-खामोर	ah-atnil-min listil-khamor
बोतल की खोलो	open the bottle
इफ़्ताह-इल-क़ान्निनाह	Iftah-il-qanninah
क्या यहाँ रात के खाने का इन्तज़ाम है ?	is dinner served here ?
हसत अकिल हनी ?	hast akil hnee ?
रात का खाना तैयार है	dinner is ready
अल-आहशा हादिर	al-ahsha hadir
कृपया मुझे लिस्ट दीजिए	please give me the list
आह-आतनिल लिस्टी-आह	ah-atnil liste-ah
फ्लोर शो किस समय शुरू होगा ?	what time does the floor show begin ?
इम्मिति-आ-यिबतिदि इल आरद ?	emmite-ah-yibtidi il ardh ?
कितनी शानदार सेटिंग है !	what a marvellous setting !
मनाज़िर इलमसरा गामीला गिदन	mana-zir i'masarah gami ila gidan
कौन गा रहा है ?	who is singing ?
मेन योगैनि ?	maen yogaenni ?

क्या मैं यह नृत्य देख सकता हूँ ?
हैल तंसमाहि लि बिहैज़िहि ऐल
रक्सा ?

may I have this dance ?
hael taes mahi li bihaezihi ael
raksa ?

क्या आप नाच्ना चाहते ?
हैल तैरकोसिन ?

would you like to dance ?
hael taerkosin ?

क्या यहाँ पर कोई डिस्कोथिक हैं ?

is there a discotheque any
where here ?

हैल तुगैद माराकिस होना ?

hael tugaed marakis hona ?

हम नाचने के लिए कहाँ जा सकते है ?
ऐयनै योमकिन ऐल ज़िहेव लिल
रक्स ?

where can we go for dancing ?
aeynae yomkin ael zihaeb lil
raks ?

आप और क्या चाहते है ?
व माथा तुरीद ऐदन ?

what else do you want ?
wa matha toreed aidhan ?

कृपया मेरे लिए बिल ले आओ
मिन फादलीक (यिब्ली) या आतनिल
हिसाब

please bring me the bill
min fadhlek (yible) or atnil
hisab

खुशी से जनाब ।
बिकोल सोरूर या सयीदी ।

with pleasure, sir
bikol soroor ya sayeedi

देर मत करना ।
ला ता अख-खीर

don't be late
laa ta akh-khir

Lesson 28

At the doctor
डाक्टर के पास

मैं अच्छा महसूस नहीं कर रहा हूँ	I am not feeling well
आ-आय-चौऊफ़ नफ़सि मोब साहि	a-ah chouf nafsi mob sahi
क्या आप मेरे लिए एक डाक्टर का प्रबन्ध कर सकते है ?	can you get me a doctor ?
श्रोतलोब लि दोक्तोर मिन फदलक ?	otlob li doktor min fadlak ?
मैं डाक्टर को मिलना चाहता हूँ	I want to see a doctor
विदिद आ-आह-चौऊफ़ दाख़तार	widdi a-ah-chouf dakhtar
डाक्टर यहाँ किस समय आ सकता है ?	what time can the doctor come ?
मैते यासतति ग्रैल दोक्तोर ग्रैल होदूर ?	maetae yastati ael doktor ael hodur ?
सुबह की नमस्ते, डाक्टर साहब	good morning, doctor
सबाहल ख़ैर या दाख़तार	sabahel kheir ya dakhtar
मुझे अच्छी तरह नींद नहीं आती	I don't sleep well
आ-बा-नाशि कवि यिस	mah-bah-nashi kwi yis
मेरी पीठ में दर्द होता है	I have a pain in the back
दा-री-बी-योह गा-नी	dah-ree bee yoh gah-nee

शायद ग्रापको ठंड लग गई है	perhaps yon caught cold
रूब्बमा तकून ग्रखज-त बर्दन	robbama takoon akhaza-ta bardan
हो सकता है, ऐसा हो	it may be so
युम्किन थालि-क	youmkin thalek
क्या ग्राप को यह शिकायत काफ़ी समय से है ?	have you this trouble since a long time ago ?
हल सार लक हाजा मिन जमनिन तबील ?	hal sar lak haja min zamnin taweel ?
क्या ग्राप मुझे कोई ऐसी चीज दे सकते है जिससे दर्द को ग्राराम मिले ?	can you give me something to relieve the pain ?
ति-दार तिद दी नी मूसक-ज्किन ?	ti-dahr tid-dee nee moosak-kin ?
ग्रब ग्राप कैसा महसूस करते है ?	how do you feel now ?
माजा तशग्ररूल ग्रान ?	ma za tashrul an ?
कोई भी सुधार नहीं हुग्रा है	there is no improvement
मा-फीश ता हास सुन	mah-feesh ta hahs-sun
क्या मुझे हस्पताल जाना पड़ेगा ?	do I have to go to the hospital
ला-जिम ग्रा रुह मुस-ताश फ़ा ?	la-zim ah rooh mus-tash-fa ?
मुझे हस्पताल ले चलो	take me to the hospital
इखियनि इलाल-मुस्ता शफ़्री ग्राह	ikhithini ilal mustashfe-ah
मुझे सिर दर्द है	I have a headache
ग्रनदी वगाह फी रूस्ती	andee wuggah fee russee
पेट दर्द	stomach ache
विजा-ग्राह (या विया-ग्राह) बातिन	wija-ah (or wiya-ah) batin

क्या डाक्टर मुझे यहाँ देखने आ सकता है ?	could the doctor come to see me here ?
हैल यसतति ग्रैल दोकतोर ग्रैल कैशफ अल्लाया होना	hael yastati ael doktor ael kaeshf allayya hona
वह बेहोश हो गई है	she has fainted
ओर-मा-ले-हा	ohr-maa-lay-ha
डाक्टर को बुलाओ	get a doctor
ओतलोब दोकतोर	ot ob doktor
मेरे दांत में दर्द है	I have a toothache
इन्दि ग्रैलैम फि ग्रैसनेनि	indi aelaem fi aesnaeni
मसूढ़ें से खून बह रहा है	the gum is bleeding
ग्रैल लैंसे तैनजिफ़	ael laesae taenzif
यह दांत दर्द कर रहा है	this tooth hurts
ई्जिहि ग्रैल सिनें तो लिमोनि	haezihi ael sinnae to limoni
मुझे दवाई कब लेनी चाहिए ?	when should I take the medicine ?
इम-ता ग्रा-खुद इद दावा ?	em-tah ah-khud id dawa ?
देन में दो बार	twice a day
मार-रि तायन फ़िल्ल योम	mah-ri tayn fill yohm
एक चम्मच भरा हुआ	a tea spoonf
मा-ला-अ सूरिया-रा	ma-lah-a seoriyah-rah
गोलियाँ	the pills
इल-होह-बूब	el hoh-boob
बिस्तर पर जाते समय	on going to bed
अब-लि-इन-नोम	ab li-in-nohm

मुझे आंखों की दवाई की भी छोटी शीशी चाहिए	I also want a small bottle of eye-drops
उरीद ऐदन जुजा जत क़तरा सग़ीरा	oreed aidan zojajat katra saghira
और कुछ ग्रायोडीन पट्टी और रूई भी	and also some iodine, gauze and cotton
ब ऐदन ब॒अज सब्बालि यूतिद वश्शाशि वल क़ुल्न ।	wa aidan ba-aj sabgali yotid washa-shi wal qotton

Lesson 29

Conversational Sentences
बातचीत वाक्य

‌बह् की नमस्ते	good morning
‌बाहिल ख़ैर	sabahil kheir
‌भ दिन	good day
‌बाहख-कूम बिल हिरी	subahkh-koom bil hiree
‌घर आओ (पुल्लिग)	come here (m.)
‌ा-आह-अल-हनी	ta-ah-al-hnee
‌झे कुछ चीज़ें चाहिएँ ।	I need some things
‌नाह आ-विज़ शवि-यित हा-गात (पुल्लिग)	a-nah ah-wiz shwi-yit ha-gat (m.)
‌नाह-ओव ज़ा शवि-यित हा-गात (स्त्रीलिग)	a-nah ow-zah shwi-yit ha-gat (f.)
‌यर आओ (स्त्रीलिग)	come here (f.)
‌ा-आह आले-हनी	ta-ah alay-hnee
‌पया अन्दर आइए	come in, please
‌द-होल, मिन-फदलक	od-hol, min fadlak
‌झे आपसे मिलकर बहुत खुशी हुई	I am very pleased to meet you
‌शरेफना	taesharafna
‌पया थोड़ा आहिस्ता बोलिए (स्त्रीलिग)	please speak slowly more (f.)
‌न फ़ादलीख त्कालमीमे आह-आला -आह-तीख	min fadhlekh tkalmemay ah-ala-sa-ah-tekh

मुझे माफ़ कीजिए	excuse me
इस्माहलि	ismahli
आप कैसे हैं ?	how are you ?
कैयफ़ै हेलिक ?	kaeyfae haelik ?
क्या आप समझते हैं ?	do you understand ?
इन्ता फाह-हीम ?	enta fah-hem ?
कृपया थोड़ा आहिस्ता बोलिए (पुल्लिंग)	please speak more slowly (m.)
मिन फ़ादलीक तीकाल्लम आह आला-सा-आह-आ	min fadhlek takallam ah-ala sa-ah-a
कोई बात नहीं	never mind
मा-लिश	ma-lish
किसी से मत कहिए	don't mention it
ईल-उफ़ू	el-uffoo
रेलगाड़ी यहाँ कितनी देर रुकती है ?	how long does the train stop here ?
इल बुब्बूर योकुफ़ हीनीर आहद्दे ए ?	el-bubbor yok kuff henner a dday ay ?
रेलगाड़ी सीटी बजा रही है	the train is whistling
अल कुईटार यासफीर	al qitar yasfer
क्या करना चाहिए ?	what is to be done ?
वा कीफ़ इलनामल ?	wa keef ilnamal ?
मुझे बहुत देर हो रही है	I am very late
अना मुता आखिर जिद्दन	ana mutah akhir jiddan

मुझे खुशी है (स्त्रीलिंग)	I am glad (f.)
अना-फ़रहानीह या अना मसरूराह	ana farhanєh or ana masroorah
जल्दी करो वरना गाड़ी के लिए हम लेट हो जाएँगे	hurry up or we shall be late for the train
अस्सिरह वा इला ताह-अख़ारना अन अल क़ितार	assrih wa ila tah-akharna an al qitar
मुझे दस लीटर पेट्रोल और कुछ तेल चाहिए ।	I want ten litres of petrol and some oil
ओव्ज़ आहशरा लीटरू पैट्रोल वीह शवाह-यीत-येत	owz ahshara leetroo petrohl weh shwah-yet-yayt
मुझे खुशी है (पुल्लिंग)	I am glad (m,)
अना-फ़हरान या अना मसरूर	ana-farhan or ana masroor
मैं नहीं दे सकता	I cannot pay
अना ला अकदर अदफा	ana la akdar ad:a
ठीक है	okay
ति-यिब	ti-yib
गुस्सा मत करो	don't be angry
ला तकुन ज़ा लान	laa takun za laan
यह चैक ले लो कैश नहीं है	take this cheque, I do not have cash
ख़ुद शैक मान-दीख फलूस	khud shaek man-deesh faloos
कितनी दयाजनक	what a pity
या खसारा	ya khsara
आपका पेशा क्या है ?	what is your profession ?
शू मिहनतक ?	shoo mihnatak ?

मैं क्लर्क हूँ — I am a clerk
अन्ना कातिब — annakaatib

उसका पेशा कौन सा है ? — what is his profession ?
शू शुगलुह ? — shoo shughluh ?

वह लेखक है — he is an author
हुवा मुहाल्लिफ — huwa muhallif

भूलिए मत (स्त्रीलिंग) — don't forget (f.)
ला तिनसेन या लेकून न तीन्सेन — la tinsain or laykoon tensain

मैं तुम्हें बाद में मिलूंगा — see you later
इलैल लिका — ilael lika

मुझे गुस्सा मत दिलाओ — do not make me angry
ला तुग़दिबनि — la tugdibni

रास्ता दिखाओ — lead the way
इमिश जिद्दामि — imish jiddami

भूलिए मत (पुर्लिंग) — don't forget (m.)
ला तिन्सी-ग्राह या लेकून तीन्सी-ग्राह — la tinse-ah or leykoon tense-ah

मुझे अकेला छोड़ दो — leave me alone
इतरोकनि लिहेलि — itrokni lihaeli

दूर चले जाओ — go away
इनसारिफ — insarif

मत जाओ — don't go
ला तरूह — la taruh

कृपया बैठ जाओ — sit down please
त्फ़ादल ऊक़ुहुद — tafadhal uqhud

दावराजा खोलो (तुम स्त्रीलिंग)	open the door (you, f.)
बातिलि-ग्राह-इलबाब **या** इफ़्ताहिल बाब	batili-ah-elbab **or** iftahil **bab**
यह जरूरी है	it is important
इन्नैहो मोहिम	innaeho mohim
मेरी चाबी गुम हो गई है	I have lost my key
मुफ़ताही दा श्रा	muftaahee daa ah
श्रापकी सेवा के लिए बहुत-बहुत धन्यवाद	thank you very much for you hospitality
श्रल्ला युज़ीदिक मिन्एल खैंर	alla yuzeedik minel khair
धीरे-धीरे	by and by
श्राहन करीब	ahan qareeb
दरवाजा खोलो (तुम पुल्लिंग)	open the door (you, m.)
बातिल-ग्राह-इलबाब **या** इफ़्ताहील बाब	batil-ah-elbab **or** iftahel **bab**
परवाह मत करो	don't bother
मुश महिमा	mush muhimah
श्रपने कपड़े पहनो	dress yourself
इलबस तहियाबक	elbas thiyaabak
कितने ?	how many ?
काम ?	kam ?
रुक जाइए कृपया	stop please
ऊकुफ़ मिन फ़ादलीक	ookuff min fadhlek

करया मुझे रास्ता दिखाओ	please show me the way
मिन फादलक वारीनी इस-सिक-का (पुल्लिंग)	min fahdluk wahree nee is-sikka (m)
मिन फादलिक वारीनी इस-सिक-का (स्त्रीलिंग)	min fahdlik wahree-nee is-sikka (f)
क्या तुम मुझे समझ सकते हो ? (तुम स्त्रीलिंग)	can you (f) understand me ?
हाल तिफ्ह्मीन शगूल ?	hal tifhmeen shagoul ?
चलते जाइए	go on
युल्लाहख	yullahkh
इस बैग को अपनी पीठ पर लादो	carry this bag on your back
इहमिल हादा-अल-कीस आह-आला ज़हारक	ihmil hadha-al-kees ah-ala zahark
क्या तुम समझते हो ?	do you understand ?
अैन्ता फा-हिम ?	enta fah-him ?
डाक्टर घर पर नही था	the doctor was not at home
लाम याकुन इल दाबीब फिन-बैत	lam yakun il dabeeb fil-bait
मैं तुम्हारी मदद कर दूँ	let me help you
खालिनि-आह-ईनक	khalini-ah-enak
मैं उसे कितना दूँ ?	how much shall I pay him ?
काम यजिब आन अदफ़ाह लाहो ?	kam yajib an adfah laho ?
क्या तुम मुझे समझ सकते हो ? (तुम पुल्लिंग)	can you (m) understand me ?
हाल तिफ्ह्हाम शगून ?	hal tifham shagoul ?
खुशी के साथ जनाब	with pleasure, sir
बिकोल सोरूर या सयीदी	bikol soroor ya sayeedi

वह कैसी है ?	how is she ?
कीफ हाल्हा ?	keef haalha ?
उसने (पुल्लिग) मुझे मारा	he hit me
हुव्वा दरबा	huwwa darba
बधाई हो	congratulations
तबरीकात	tabreekaat
हम आपके एहसानमन्द है	we are much obliged to you
मशकुरीन वायीद	mashkureen wayed
शायद बारिश हो	it may rain
रूब्बामा तमतुर	rubbama tamtur
तुम कैसे हो ?	how do you do ?
इजिगायुक ?	izzigh yuck ?
धीरे	slowly
बीशवेश	beshwaysh
ध्यान रखिए	take care
हुली-व्राहल्लुक	hulle-bahluck
मैं कृतज्ञ हूँ	I am obliged
आना ममनून	ana mamnoon
ध्यान रखना (तुम स्त्रीलिंग)	watch out (you, f)
इन्ताबे	intabhay
क्या यह जगह खाली है ?	is this place free ?
इल-माहुल्ल दा फ़ऊदी ?	el-mahull dah fudee ?
यह बहुत सुन्दर हैं, क्या यह नहीं है ?	it is very beautiful, isn't it ?
होन्नीर कव्राह-यिस कीत्तीर	henner kwah-yis ketter,
मूश कीद्दा ?	moosh kedda ?

थियेटर कहाँ है ?	where is the theatre ?
अल मसरा-वीन ?	al masrah-ween ?
दायें को मुड़ो	turn to the right
खुद यामीनक	khudh yameenak
ध्यान रखना (तुम पुल्लिग)	watch out (you m)
इन्तीबीह	intebeh
मुझे स्टेशन ले चलो	take me to the station
खुदनि लिल-महात्ताह	khudhni lil-mahattah
पुलिस को बुलाओ	call the police
ओतलोब अेल बोलिस	otlob ael bolis
मुझे एक गिलास पानी चाहिए	I want a glass of water
उरीद कास मा	Urid kas ma
मेरे लिए इन्तज़ार करो	wait for me
(तुम स्त्रीलिंग)	(you, f)
कानि बायीख या ईन्तादरीनि	kani bayeekh or intadhreeni
तुम कौन हो ?	who are you ?
मीन अैन्ति ?	meen enti ?
एक मिनट रुको	stop for a moment
उसबुर लहज़ाह	usbur lahzah
तुम किस देश के हो ?	which country are you from ?
इन्ती मिन अय्य बैलद ?	inti min ayy balad ?
मैं एक भारतीय हूँ	I am an Indian (m)
अना हिन्दी	ana hindee
मेरे लिए इन्तज़ार करो (तुम पुल्लिग)	wait for me (you m)
कानि बायीक या इन्तीदर्नि	kani bayeek or intedhrni

मुझे बहुत देर हो चुकी थी — I was very late

आना कुन्तु मुत्हा खिरें जिद्दान — aana kuntu mutha khiran jiddan

कितना ? — how much ?

बी-काम ? — bee-kam ?

मैं तुम्हें यकीन दिलाता हूँ — I assure you

आना ऊहाक़्क़िक़ लक — aana uhaqqiq lak

यह (स्त्रीलिंग) बहुत सुन्दर हैं — it (f) is very beautiful

वायीद जामीलह या वायीद हिल्वाह — wayeed jamelah or wayeed hilwah

चुप हो जाओ — be quiet

इह्दा — ihda

अब जाने का समय हो गया हैं — it is time to go

हाना-प्रल-दहाब — hana-al-dahab

यह खुशी की बात है — it is a pleasure

हादा वाजिब — hadha wajib

हर तरह से — by all means

माहलूम — mahloom

यह (पुल्लिंग) बहुत सुन्दर है — it (m) is very beautiful

वायीद जमील या वायीद हिलो — wayeed jamel or wayeed hilow

मैं अशोका होटल में ठहरा हुआ हूँ — I am staying at the Ashoka hotel

आना नाज़िल फ़ि ऊतील अशोका — ana nazil fi uteel Ashoka

क्या तुम पढ़ सकते हो ? — can you read ?

ऐंता तक़दार तक़रा ? — enta taqdar taqra ?

घर के ग्रन्दर	in the house
फिल बयत	fil -bayt
खाना स्वादिष्ट है	the food is delicious
इल-ग्राह ग्रकल लादीद	il ah akl ladeed
मैं यह बाला लूँगा	I will take this one
ग्राकुद हादि	akudh hadhi
मैं ऐसा नही सोचता	I don't think so
ला-आह-प्रताक़िद थालीक	la-ah-ataqid thalek
बहाँ तुम हो	there you are
इत्फा-द-दालु	itfad dalu
शौचालय कहाँ है ?	where is the toilet ?
इल-कुन्नीफ़ फेन ?	el-kunneef fayn ?
तुम क्या इस्तेमाल करते हो ?	what do you use ?
माथा तस्तामिल ?	matha tasta mil ?
बह (स्त्रीलिंग) वास्तव में ग्राभारी है	she is really grateful
हिया शकुराह हक़ीकत	hiya shakurah haqikat
तुम्हें मुझे बताना चाहिए था	you should have told me
कान मिनल वाजिब ग्रन तख़िबरनी	kan miral waib an takhibrni
तुम शायद यह पसन्द करो	you may like it
रूद्यामा तुहिब्बुन	rubbama tuhibbul
क्या ग्रापके पास कोई सिगरेट है ?	do you have any cigarette ?
ग्रिन्दक सकाइर ?	indak saka ir ?

आप यहाँ कैसे आए ?	how did you come here ?
कैफ अतैत हुना ?	keif ateit huna ?
मुझे अफसोस है कि मैं आपको तकलीफ दे रहा हूँ	I am sorry to trouble you
अन्ना आसिफ लिम-दि-ऐ-तक	anah asif lim di-ay-tak
वह (स्त्रीलिंग) इंतजार कर सकती है	she can wait
हिया तस्तातीह आन तसबुर	hiya tastateeh an tasbur
मैं काफी चाय ला रहा हूँ	I am bringing the coffee tea
आना जाय बिल-कहवा चे	aana jaya bil qahwa chay
वह अच्छा आदमी है	he is a nice fellow
हु जादा तैयिब	hu jada taiyib
ये अण्ड खराब है	these eggs are bad
इल-बैद दी मोश कवाह-यिस	el-bayd dee most kwah-yis
मैं क्या करूं ?	what shall I do ?
शु आह मल ?	shoo ahmal ?
मुझे आपने साथ ले चलो	take me with you
फूदनि माहक	fudhni mahak
तुमने अच्छा काम किया	you have done well
फ़ा आह-अल्ता हसानन	fa ah-alta hasanan
एकदम चाय बनवाओ	get the tea ready at once
हादिरिश शै हाला	haddirish shai hala
ध्यान पूर्वक रहो	be careful
इन्ताबि	intabi
नहीं वहाँ पर नही है	no there isn't
मा-फी	ma-fee

मैं हैरान हूं	I am astonished
श्राना मुताह्-श्राज्जिब	aana mutah-ajjib
क्या तुम गाङ॑ हो ?	are you the guard ?
इन्ता इल-हाह॒रीस्स ?	enta el-hahress ?
यह सड़क कहाँ जाती है ?	where does this road lead ?
इस-सिक-का दी-ती-वादी श्रा-ला फेन ?	is-sik-kah dee-tee wahdee ah-lah fayn ?
कृपया करके वाद में श्राना	please come back later
मिन फादलिक ता श्रा-लीका मान शवीया	min fahdlik ta ah-leeka man shwiyah
मुभ्से गुम गया है (यदि कारक स्त्रीलिंग हो)	I have lost it (if the object is f.)
दा-श्र॑ह या श्राह-ता-श्राहा	dha-ah ya ah-ta-ah-ha
मैं तुम्हें तकलीफ नहीं देना चाहता था	I did not like to trouble you
॰लम उहिब्बु इज॒श्राजक	lam ohibbu izajak
ठीक है, श्राश्रो चलें	well let us go
हसनन हय्या बिना	hassanan haya bina
मुभे एक मोमवत्ती की जरूरत है	I need a candle
श्राह-श्राविज शमाह	ah-ayiz shamah
शोर मत मचाश्रो	don't make a noise
ला ताह॒मल ज॒ैताह	la tahmal zaitah
मेरे लिए कुर्सी लाश्रो	bring me a chair
हात लि कुर्सी	hat li kursi
इसको रोको	stop it
वकिफ हूँ	waqqef hoo

बोलो	speak
तकल्लम	takallam
मुझ से गुम हो गया है (यदि कारक पुल्लिंग हो)	I have lost it (if the object is m.)
दा-आह-या-आह-ताह	dha-ah-ya-ah-tah
मुझे एक प्रवेश परमिट चाहिए	I want an entry permit
अना आविज़ तसरीह अद-दुखुल	ana aawiz tasreeh ad-dukhool
हमें वापिस कुवैत ले चलो	drive us back to Kuwait
ओहद बिना इला कुवैत	ohd bina ila Kuwait
नौकर को बुलाओ	call the servant
इन्दाह-इल-खाद्दम	indah-il-khaddam
क्या मेरे लिए कोई चिट्टी है ?	are there any letters for me ?
फीख गवाह बाहत उश-शाहनी ?	feekh gawah baht ush-shahnee ?

Glossary

Books and stationery
पुस्तकें तथा लेखन सामग्री

शब्दकोष	क़ामूस	qamous	dictionary
पुस्तक	किताब	kitaeb	book
पेन	कलम हिब्र	kalam hibr	pen
पेंसिल	कलम रोसास	kalam rosas	pencil
गोंद	अहमर	ahmar	gum
बाल पेन	कलम हिब्र गेफ	kalam hibr gaef	ballpoint pen
कागज	वर्क़	warq	paper
स्याही	हिब्र	hibr	ink
कार्बन कागज	वरक कारबोन	warak karbon	carbon paper
स्याही चूस	नशाफ़	nashafa	blotting paper
रजिस्टर	सिजिल	sijil	register
रेखाचित्र कागज	वरक रैसम	warak raesm	drawing paper
नक्शा	खरिता	kharita	map
रबर	मिम्हात	mimhat	rubber
स्याही की दवात	मिह्बरा	mihbara	inkpot
स्लेट	लोहु हजर	lohu hajar	slate

चाक	तब्शूर	**tab**shur	chalk
फुटा	मसतरा	mastara	ruler
लिखने वाला पैंड	वलॉक वरक	blok warak	writing pad
लिफाफा	जर्फ़	zarf	envelope
सहायक किताब	दलील	daleel	guide-book
कापी	कशकुल	kashkul	note-book
डायरी	मदहाक्किरा	madhakkira	diary

The colours

रंग

बेंगनी	बनाफ़साजि	banafsaji	violet
गहरा नीला	नीली	neely	indigo
हरा	अख़्दर	akhdar	green
नारंगी	बुरतृक़ानि	burtuqani	orange
लाल	अहमर	ahmar	red
गुलाबी	क़िर्मज़ी	qirmazy	pink
पीला	अस्फर	asfar	yellow
सफेद	अब्यद	abyad	white
भूरा	अस्मर	asmar	brown
स्लेटी	अशहब	ash-hab	grey
काला	असवद	aswad	black
नीला	अज़रक़	azraq	blue
सुनहरी	ज़हबी	zahbee	golden

ग्रासमानी	समावि	samawi	sky-blue
जामुनी	ग्रोजंवानी	orjwani	purple
कच्चा रंग	लौनुन ब्राहित	loanun bahit	fade colour
गहरा रंग	लौनुन ग़ामिद	loanun ghamid	dark colour
हल्का रंग	लौनुन फ़ातीह	loanun fateeh	light colour
पक्का रंग	लौनुन साबित	loanun sabit	fast colour

Flowers
फूल

लाला (ट्यूलिप)	खोज़ामा	khozama	tulip
चमेली	यासमीन	yasmeen	jasmine
गुलाब	वर्द	ward	rose
सदाबहार फूलों की बेल	कामीलिया	kameelia	cameelia
...रगिस	नर्जिस	narjiss	narcissus
...ली	ज़न्बाक	zanbaq	lily
बनफ़शा	बनफ़सज	banafsaj	violet
गुलनार	क़रून फुल	quoronful	carnation

Professions
धंधे

एकाउन्टेंट	मुहासिब	muhasib	accountant
चार्टंडं एकाउन्टेंट	मुहासिब क़ानूनी	muhasib qaanoonee	chartered accountant

इस्पैक्टर	मुफ़तिश	mufatish	inspector
स्मगलर	मुहर्रिब	muharrib	smuggler
कुली	शय्याल	shayyal	porter
गायक	मुग़न्नी	mughanne	singer
डाक्टर	तबीब	tabeeb	doctor
क्लर्क	कातिब	katib	clerk
मैनेजर	मुदीर	mudeer	manager
पाइलेट	तय्यार	tayyar	pilot, aviator
हलवाई	हुलवानी	hulwany	confectioner
बेंक कैशियर	सराफ़	saraaf	bank cashier
डाकिया	बोस्ताज़ी	bostazee	postman
सेक्रेटरी	सिकरितीरा	sikriteera	secretary
बढ़ई	नज्जार	najjaar	carpenter
इमारत बनाने वाला इन्जीनियर	मुहन्दिस मिमारी	muhandis mimary	architect
सिपाही	जुन्दि	jundi	soldier
नीलाम करने वाला	दल्लाल	dallal	auctioneer
राजदूत	सफ़ीर	safeer	ambassador
लेखा-परीक्षक (आडिटर)	मुदक़िक़ हिसाबात	mudaqiq hisabat	auditor
वकील	मुहामि	muhami	advocate, lawyer
अभिनेता	मुमाथिल	mumathil	actor
अभिनेत्री	मुमथिला	mumathila	actress

कान की बीमारियों का डाक्टर	तबीब अथान	tabeeb athan	aurist
किताबें बेचने वाला	कुतबी	kutbee	bookseller
हिसाब किताब रखने वाला	मासिक दफ़ातिर	masik dafatir	bookkeeper
नाई	हल्लाक़	hallaq	barber
जिन्द साज	मुजाल्लिद कुतुब	mujallid kutub	bookbinder
लुहार	हद्दाद	haddad	blacksmith
राजगीर	बन्ना	banna	brick layer
कसाई	लह्हाम	lahham	butcher
व्यापारी, दुकानदार	ताजिर	tajir	businessman merchant
दलाल	सिमसार	simsar	broker
नान बाई, बेकर	ख़ब्बाज़	khabbaz	baker
छुरी-चाकू बेचने वाला	सकाकीनी	sakakenee	cutler
दवाईयां बेचने वाला	किमावि	kimawi	chemist
सिविल इन्जीनियर	मुहन्दिस मदनी	muhandis madni	civil engineer
कंडक्टर	कौम-सारी	kom-saree	conductor
रसोइया	तब्वाख	tabbaakh	cook
ड्राइबर	सोव-वा	sow-wa	driver
डायरेक्टर	मुखरिज़	mukhrij	director
दांतों का डाक्टर	तबीब अस्नान	tabeeb asnan	dentist
औषध-विक्रेता	सैदली	saidaly	druggist

रंगसाज	सब्बाग़	sabbagh	dyer
नक्शा बनाने वाला	रस्साम	rassam	draughtsman
नृत्य करने वाला या वाली	रक्क़ासा	raqqasa	dancer
इंजीनियर	मुहन्दिस	muhandis	engineer
सम्पादक	रा इस-तहरीर	ra is-tahreer	editor
इलेक्ट्रिकल इन्जीनियर	मुहन्दिस कहरबाई	muhandis kahrabai	electrical engineer
मछेरा	सम्माक	sammak	fisher
घोड़ों का डाक्टर	बीतार	beetar	farrier
ग़ाईड	दलील	deleel	guide
गार्ड	हारिस	haris	guard
गवर्नर	हाकिम	hakim	governor
सुनार	सयोग़	ayegh	goldsmith
पन्सारी	सम्मान	samman	grocer
सब्ज़ी वाला	खोदहारी	khodhary	green-grocer
सेविका	मुदिफ़ा	mudifa	hostess
दुभाषिया	तुर्जुमान	turjuman	interpreter
जज	कादी	kadee	judge
कठिहार	नज्जर दिक्क़ो.	najjar diqqi	joiner
जौहरी	जवाहिरजी	jawahirjee	jeweller
पत्रकार	सुहुफ़ि	suhufi	journalist
ताले बनाने वाला	सनि अक़फ़ाल	sani aqfal	locksmith
लाइब्रेरियन	कुतुबी	kutubee	librarian

चक्की वाला	तहहान	tahhan	miller
मेकनिक्ल	मुहन्दिस	muhandis	mechanical
इन्जीनियर	मिकानिकि	mikaniki	engineer
संगीत शास्त्री	मुसीक़ी	museeqi	musician
मुद्रा बदलने वाला	सर्राफ़	sarraf	money-changer
नर्स	मुमारिदाह	mumarridah	nurse
अफसर	दाबित	daabit	officer
आपरेटर	अमिल इत तिलीफून	aamil it-tileeon	operator
हड्डियों का डाक्टर	दोक-तोर री-ज़ाम	dok-tohr ree-zahm	orthopedist
आँखों का डाक्टर	तबीब उयून	tabeeb oyoun	oculist
चित्रकार	मुसौउविर	musowwir	painter
छापने वाला	तब्बाह	tabbah	printer
प्रोफेसर	उस्ताद	ustad	professor
फोटोग्राफर	मुसव्विर	musawir	photographer
चिकित्सक	तबिब	tabib	physician
कवि	शायर	shair	poet
प्रोड्यूसर	मुखरिज	mukhrij	producer
पुलिस	शुराति	shurati	policeman
प्रधानाचार्य	आमिद	aamid	principal
उपदेशक	वा इथ	wa ith	preacher
रिपोर्टर	मुरासिल सोहुफि	murasil sohufil	reporter
शल्य चिकित्सक	जर्राह	jarrah	surgeon

लेखन सामग्री विक्रेता	बाए कुर्तासिया	baih kortaissia	stationer
कातने वाला	गज्जाल	ghazzal	spinner
विद्वान्	तिलमिद	tilmid	scholar
जूते बनाने वाला	सक्काफ़	sakkaf	shoemaker
नौकर	खादिम	khadim	servant
साइन बोर्ड रंगने वाला	खत्तात	khattat	sign-writer
जहाज की परिचारिका	मुदीफा	mudeefah	stewardess
अध्यापक	मुहाल्लिम	muh-allim	teacher
टीन बनाने वाला	सनकारी	sankari	tin-smith
चमड़ा रंगने वाला	दब्बाग़	dabbagh	tanner
दर्जी	कितात	kitat	tailor
टिकिट इकट्ठी करने वाला	कुमसारी	kumsaree	ticket-collector
चोर	हा-राह्-मे	hah-rah-may	thief
तम्बाकू-बेचने वाला	बाए दुखान	baih dukhan	tabacconist
अनुवादक	मुतर्जिम	mutarjim	translator
खराद का काम करने वाला	खर्रात	kharrat	turner
सोफ़ा बनाने वाला	मुनज्जिद	munijid	upholsterer

जान्वरों का डाक्टर	तबीब बैतरी	tabeeb baitary	veterinary
चौकीदार	ग़ाफ़िर	ghafir	watchman
जुलाहा	हाइक	hayek	weaver
घड़ी साज़	साह-आति	sah-ati	watch-maker
लेखक	कातिब	katib	writer
सफ़ेदी करने वाला	तर्राश	tarrash	white-washer

Agricultural Products
खेती की उपज

चावल	अरूज्ज़	aruzz	rice
सेब	तुफ़्फ़ाह	tuffaha	apple
गेहूँ	क़ुम्ह, हिन्ता	quamh, hinta	wheat
अंगूर	त्रिनब	inab	grapes
अनार	रूम्मान	rumman	pomegranate
आम	मन-गा	man-ga	mango
खजूर	बलह	balah	dates
चेरी	कराज़	karaz	cherries
आड़ू	दुर्राक़	dorraq	peaches
अंजीर	تين	teen	figs
संतरा	बुर्तूक़ाल	burtuqaal	orange
अखरोट	जोज़	jauz	walnuts

ब्रादाम	लौज़	lauz	almonds
खूबानी	मिशमिश	mishmish	apricot
नाशपाती	कात्रा	kamatra	pear
केला	मौज़	mauz	banana
नींबू	लेमून	leimoon	lemon
ब्रालुबुखारा	खौख	khoukh	plum
श्रीफल, सूरजफल	सफ़रजल	safarjal	quince
शाहबलूत	किस्तना	kistana	chestnuts
छोटा चकोतरा	लेमून हिंदी	leimoon hindee	grape-fruit
पिंगल फल	बुन्दुक़	bondoq	hazelnuts
खरबूजा	शम्माम	shammam	melon musk
तरबूज	बित्तीख	biteek	water-melon
नारियल	जौंजुल हिंद	jouzel hind	cocoanut
शहतून	तूत	toot	mulberries
किशमिश	ज़िबीब	zibeeb	raisins
मक्का	थोरा सफरा	thora safra	maize
जौ	शश्रीर	shaeer	barley
प्याज	बसल	basal	onions
टमाटर	बतातिस	bataatis	tomatoes
फूल गोभी	कर्नाबीत	qarnabeet	auliflower
ब्ररबां	फ़सुलिया	fasulia	beans (lima)
फलियां, सेम	फूल	fool	beans
सेम (हरे)	लुबीह	lubieh	beans (green)
ब्रालू	बताता	batata	potato

मटर	बाज़ोल्ला	bazolla	peas
चुकन्दर	सिल्क़	silq	beet
बन्द गोभी	मलफ़ूफ़	malfoof	cabbages
मूली	फ़िजिली-ग्राह	fijile-ah	radish
पालक	सबानीख़	sbanekh	spinach
चने	हुम्मुस	hommos	chick-peas
सीताफल	यक़तिना	yaqtina	pumpkin
लहसुन	थोम	thoom	garlic
मसूर की दाल	ग्रदस्स	adass	lentils
खीरा	ख़िग्रार	khiar	cucumber
सलाद	ख़ास	khass	lettuce
काली मिर्च	फ़लाफ़िल	falafil	peppers
शकरकन्दी	शमन्दर	shamandar	beet-root
ग्रजवाइन	करफिस	karafs	celery
बैंगन	बथीन जान	bathenjan	egg-fruits
कद्दू	कुराग्र	quarah	squash
पुदीना	नाना	nana	mint
सौंफ	यासून	yasoon	aniseed
लौकी	कौसा	kousa	marrows
गन्ना	क़सबु सुक्कर	qasbu sukkar	sugarcane
करौंदा	कुज़बरा	kuzbara	gooseberry
कपास	क़ुत्न	qutn	cotton

अफ़ीम	अफ़्यून	afyoun	opium
चीनी	शिकार	shikar	sugar

Food and Drinks
खाने तथा पीने की वस्तुएँ

अंडा	बेदा	baida	egg
दूध	हलीब	haleeb	milk
मछली	समक	samak	fish
पानी	मा	maa	water
शराब	अरक	arak	liquor
हिस्की	अल-वीसकी	al-weeskee	whisky
केक	काक	kak	cake
आइस क्रीम	इसक-रयम	isk-raym	ice-cream
मक्खन	ज़िब-दा	zib-da	butter
सैंडविच	सन-दा-बितश	san da witsh	sandwitch
क्रीम	ज़िबदिह	zibdih	cream
सूअर का मांस	लहम ख़िन्ज़ीर	laham khinzeer	bacon
गाय का मांस	लहम बक़र	laham baqar	beef
भेड़ का मांस	लामा गनाम	lama ghanam	mutton
बर्फ	थालज	thalj	ice
नींबू जल	लेमुन	laymun	lemonade
मीट	लाहम	laham	meat

चटनी	सलसाह	salsah	sauce
सन्तरे का रस	ब्रा सीर बोर तू ब्रन	ah seer bohr too an	orange juice
सिरक	खल्ल	khall	vinegar
काफ़ी	क़ाहवा	qahwah	coffee
चाय	शैं	shai	tea
मवखन	जुहदा	zuhdah	butter
रोटी	खुबज़	khubz	bread
नमक	मिल्ह	milh	salt
सूप	शूरबा	shoorbah	soup
मुरब्वा	मुरब्बा	murabba	jam
बीयर	बिरी-ब्राह या बीब्रर	bire-ah or beer	beer
पनीर	जिब्नीह	zibneh	cheese
बिस्कुट	बुक़सुमात	buqsumat	biscuits
शराब	खामोर	khamor	wine
मीट का सूप	शोरवित लेहुम	shorbit laehm	meat-soup
अंगूरों का रस	ब्रा-सीर ए नब	a-seer ay nab	grape juice
चीनी	शिकार	shikar	sugar
भुना हुब्रा गाय का मांस	लाहम मशवि	laham mashwi	roast beef
फ्ल का रस	ब्रा सीर फा वा किह	a-seer fa wa keh	fruit juice

उबले हुए ग्रंडे	बायद मस लू	bayd mas loo	boiled eggs
टोस्ट	मुहम्मास	muhammas	toast
ग्रामलेट	इग-गा	eg-gah	omelette
चिग्म	ली-बान	lee·ban	chewing gum
कलेजा	चब्दिद	chabdid	liver
टमाटर का सूप	शोर बित ता मा-	shor bit ta	tomato-soup
	तिम	mah-tim	

Household Utensils
घरेलू बर्तन

स्टोव	मौक़िद	mauqid	stove
प्लेट	तबक़	tabaq	plate
चमचा	मि लक़ा	mi laqa	spoon
चाक़ू	सिकीन	sikkeen	knife
कांटा	शूका	shookah	fork
प्याला	फिनजान	finjaan	cup
लैम्प	मिसबा	misbah	lantern
तन्दूर	फर्न	furn	oven
चायदानी	इब्रिक़ शाइ	ibriq shay	teapot
गिलास	कूब	kub	tumbler
थरमस बोतल	तिरमोस	tirmos	thermos flask
चीनी के बर्तन	ग्रतबाक़	atbaq	crockery
ट्रे	सिनिया	sinniya	tray

बाल्टी	सातिल	satil	**pail**
झाड़ू	मिकनिसा	miknisah	**broom**
टोकरी	सा-बत	sa-bat	basket
बोतल खोलने वाला	मिफ़ताह लिग़राश	miftah lighrash	bottle **opener**
बर्तन	जिदिर	jidir	pan
तश्तरी	सान सग़ीर	sahan sgheer	saucer
कुल्हाड़ी	बलता	balta	axe
टार्च	बत्तारिय्या	battariyya	torch
फ्रिज	बररद या थालाजीह्	barrad or thallajeh	refrigerator
टोस्टर	मिह्लयिल खुबिज	mehlayil khubiz	toaster
चाय का चमचा	मिलग्रक़त शाइ	milaqat shay	teaspoon
जग	इब्रीक़	ibreeq	jug
खाने का चमचा	मिग्रक़त तमाम	milaqat tmaam	tablespoon
शीशी	गारशीह्	gharsheh	bottle
तलने का बर्तन	मिक़ला	miqla	frying **pan**
छलनी	मिनखाल	minkhal	sieve
मटका	ब्रीग	breeg	pitcher
कॉर्क निकालने वाला यन्त्र	मुफ़्ताह क़नानि	muftah qanani	cork-screw
मेज	तवलीह् या तवीला	tawleh or tawila	table
नमकदानी	मिम्लाह	mimlaha	salt-cellar
कुर्सी	कुर्सी	kursi	chair

कैंची	मीक़ास	meqas	scissors
चीनीदानी	सुक्करिय	sukkariya	sugar-basin
कबाब का सीखचा	सीख	seekh	spit
अण्डा फेंटने का बर्तन	मिख्फक़त बैद	mikhfaqat beidh	egg-whisk
सुई	इब्रीह	ibreh	needle
प्रेस	मिकवाह	mikwah	iron
कीप	मीह्क़ान	mehqan	funnel
सूप प्लेट	सह्न शोरबा	sahn shorba	soup-plate
डोगा, प्लेट	जात	jat	dish
सन्दूक	सिन्दुक़	sinduq	box
सिल	मिस्सन	missan	grindstone
ढक्कन खोलने वाला	मिफ़्ताह इलब	miftah ilab	tin opener
हथौड़ी	कस्सारत जौज़	kassarat jaz	nut cracker
मूसल	मिदक़्क़	midaqqa	pestle
ओखली	हाविन	hawin	mortar

Things of General Use
सामान्य प्रयोग की वस्तुएं

| टूथ पेस्ट | माह्जुनिल अस्नान | mah-junil asnan | tooth paste |

दांत साफ करने का ब्रश	फोरशित अल-असनान	forshit a l-asnan	tooth brush
कंघी	मुश्त	mushat	comb
साबुन	साबून	sabun	soap
थैला	किस्स	kiss	bag
तौलिया	फूतात याद	futat yad	towel
धागा	खयत	khayt	thread
जूते	अथिय	ahthia	shoes
सेंडलें	सन-दल्ल	san-dull	sandals
शेव करने वाला साबुन	साबुनिल-हिलाक़ा	sabunil-hilaqa	shaving-soap
ब्लेड	अमवास हिलाक़ा	amwas hilaqa	razor blades
छतरी	शाम-सी-या	sham-see-ya	umbrella
सिगरेट	जिगायीर	jigayer	cigarettes
सिगरेट रखने वाला डिब्बा	इलबित संग शैयिर	ilbit saeg aeyir	cigarette case
छोटा तौलिया	फूता	futa	napkin
चप्पलें	नाल जन्नुबा	nahl zannuba	slippers
सुई	इबरा	ibra	needle
शीशा	मिरात	mirat	mirror
दियासलाई	कब रीत	kab reet	matches
बरसाती कोट	कोट-मितर	coat-mitar	rain-coat
प्लग	रशश	rashash	plug

बिजली का तार	सिल्क	silk	wire
धूप का चश्मा	नदारत शम्स	nadharat shams	goggles
रूमाल	मन्दील	mandeel	handkerchief
अंगूठी	खातिम	khatim	ring
लम्बी जुर्राबें	जरावात	jarabat	stockings
फीता	दुन-तिल-ला	dun-til-la	lace
सूती जुर्राबें	जराबात काटन	jarabat cotton	cotton stockings
बल्ब	लाम-बा	lahm-bah	bulb
कैमरे की फिल्म	फ़िल्म कामीरा-ग्राह	film kamera-ah	camera film
दस्ताने	दलग याद	dlagh yad	gloves
बटुआ	मिहफज्ञा	mihfaza	purse
धूप की छतरी	शमसिया हरिमि	shamsia harimi	parasol
ऐनक	नजारात	najarat	spectacles
अलार्म घड़ी	मि-नब-बिह	mi-nib bih	alarm clock
घड़ी	सा-इत हायत	sa-it hayt	clock
चेन	सिलसिलात	silsilat	chair
हार	ग्रोकद	okd	necklace
जेवर	ग-वा-हिर	ga-wa-hir	jewellery
रेडियो	रदयो	radyo	radio
टेप रिकार्डर	ग्रालतित तसज्ञील	aalatit taszeel	taperecorder
चाबी	मिफ़्ताह	miftah	key

स्पंज	इसफिनजा	isfinja	sponge
सेंट	इत्र	etr	perfume
सूटकेस	शुनता	shunta	suitcase
टेलीविजन सैंट	तिलफिज़्यून	tilfizyoon	television set
कैस्ट	कसिस्त	kasitt	cassette
टायलट पेपर	बा रा तो बा लित	ba ra toh ba lit	toilet paper
तेल	ज़ित	zit	oil
पंखा	मरवाहा	marwahah	fan
गेंद	कुररा	kurran	ball
फुटबाल	करातु अल-कदम	kuratu al-qadam	football
कागज के रूमाल	फवात्त ३रक	fowatt warak	paper napkin
रस्सी	खित	khit	string
मोमबत्तीयां	शैम	shaem	candles
पिन	दब्बूस	dabboos	pin
थर्मामीटर	तिरमोमितर	tirmomitr	thermometer
क्रीम	करिम	krim	cream
शैम्पू	शेमपू	shaempu	shampoo
बटन	ज़ोरार	zorar	button
जंजीर	सोसतै	sostae	jip
कानों में डालने वाले कांटे	हैलैक	haelaek —	earrings

पिस्टक	रूज़ लिल शैं फ़ेयिफ	ruzh lil shae faeyif	lipstick
लों में डालने ा तेल	ज़ित शग्रीर	zit shaer	hair oil
ऊडर	बदरा लिल वेंग	badra lil waegh	face powder
प	कोब्बा	kobbaa	hat
ी	हिज़ोम	hizaem	belt
ा	फ़ोरशैं	forshae	brush
गारु नाशक	करिम मोताहिर	krim motahhir	antiseptic
म			cream
ी	बत-ता-री-या	bat-tah-ree-yah	battery
ी	जरिस	jairs	bell
ौड़ा	शा-कूश	sha-koosh	hammer
फा	कनाबा	kanabah	sofa
योडीन	योद	yod	iodine
लाई घड़ी	सा-इत-ईद	sa-it eed	wrist watch
ड़या	ग्रा-रू-सा	aa-roo-sah	doll
लौने	ले-ग्रब	lay-ub	toys
प	गोविशैं	goweshee	strap
यर	ग्रा गा ला	aa ga la	tire
लदान	ज़ो-रो-या	zoh-ree-ya	vase
र टानिक	दहान लिश-शग्रर	dhan lish-shaar	hair tonic
ड़यां	ग्रसाविर	asawir	bracelets

अखबार	सहिफा	sahifa	newspaper
टोकरी	सल्ला	salla	basket
टाइप राइटर	अलात अल किताबा	alat al kitaba	typewriter
टिकटें	तवाबि	tawaabee	stamps
पेट्रोल	बोतरोल	betrol	petrol
कोयला	फ़ाम हजारी	fahm hajari	coal
गैस	गाज़	ghaz	gas
मिट्टी का तेल	काज	kaz	kerosene
विटामिन	वितामिनत	vitaminat	vitamin
टानिक	मुक़व्वी	muqawee	tonic
पट्टी	रिबात	ribat	bandage
मरहम	मरहम	marham	ointment
ऐश ट्रे	मिनफद हत सकायीर	minfadhat sakayer	ash-tray
चटाई	हसीरा	haseera	mat
सन्दूक	हक़िबात सफ़र	haqibat safar	trunk

Clothes
कपड़े

क़मीज	क़मीस	qamees	shirt
टोपी	कैसकितैं	kaeskittae	cap
कोट	बालतो	balto	coat
पैन्ट	बनतालून	bantaloon	trousers

स्कर्ट	तनुरा	tannura	skirt
जैकट	जकीत	jakeet	jacket
पजामा	बिजामी-ग्राह़	bijame-ah	pyjamas
जुराबें	शोराब	shorab	socks
ब्लाउज	बलुज़ी	bluzee	blouse
नकटाई	रबतात उनुक़	rabtat onoq	necktie
वास्कट	सिद्रिया	sidriya	waist-coat
रात की पोशाक	क़मीस़ नोमी	qamees nome	nightgown
स्वैटर	इसदाईरी	isdairy	sweater
नैकर	हाफ़त	hafat	shorts
ओवर कोट	मितफ़	mitaf	overcoat
फ़राक	फ़ोस्तान	fostan	frock
शाल	शाल	shal	shawl
स्कार्फ	इरदी-ग्राह़	irde-ah	scarf
सूट	बादलाह़	badleh	suit
एप्रन	मिज़ार	mizar	apron
रिब़न	शरीत	shareet	ribbon
बुर्क़ा	बुर्क़ा	burqa	veil
कम्बल	बोरनूस	bornous	blanket
चोली	हेमिल सद्र	haemil sadr	brassiere
कालर	यैका	yaeka	collar
रजाई	लिहाफ़	lehaaf	quilt
कुशन	मस नद	mas nad	cushion

चादर	बशर	bshar	sheet
तकिया	मोसिदीह	mosideh	pillow
मेजपोश	खीदरात ताव्लीह	khedrat tawleh	table cloth
गलीचा	मिज्जादा	sijjaadah	carpet
पर्दा	सितारा	sitara	curtain
तकिये का गिलाफ़	थोब्रब मोसिदीह	thoab mosideh	pillow-case
ड्रेसिंग गाऊन	रोब	rob	dressing-gown

Human Body
मानव शरीर

हाथ	याद	yad	hand
पैर	रिजिल	rijil	foot
ऊंगली	इसबी	isbe	finger
कान	इदहिन	idhin	ear
मुंह	थुम	thum	mouth
आंख	आराह-ईयन	ah-eyn	eye
जीभ	लिसान	lissan	tongue
नाक	खशिम	khashim	nose
घुटना	रिक़बाह	riqbah	knee
ठोड़ी	थिक़िन	thiqin	chin
टांग	सक़	saq	leg
कूल्हा	रैद्फ़	raedf	nip

सिर	रास	raas	head
दांत	श्रसनान	asnaan	teeth
एक दांत	सिन	sin	tooth
पीठ	जहर	zahr	back
ऐड़ी	कै ग्रैंब	kae aeb	heel
कलाई	मि सम	mi sam	wrist
पेट	बातिन	batin	stomach
कन्धा	कातिफ	katif	shoulder
चेहरा	वजह्	wajh	face
छाती	सदर	sadr	chest
बाल	शाहर	shahr	hair
अंगूठा	इबहाम	ibham	thumb
भुजा	थीरा	thira	arm
गाल	खाद्	khadd	cheek
गला	ग्रैल ज़ोर	ael zohr	throat
गर्दन	रक़ाबा	raqaba	neck
जबड़ा	फाक	fak	jaw
चमड़ी	ज़िल्द	zild	skin
माथा	जबहा	jabha	forehead
भौंहें	हाजिब्रान	hajiban	eye-brows
दिमाग	मुख	mukh	brain
होठ	शफ़ातन	shafatan	lips
कुहनी	कु	ku	elbow

टखना	कसबित ग्रैं रिग्ल	kasbit ae rigl	ankle
दिल	क़ल्ब	qalb	heart
हंड्डी	अज़म	azm	bone
पसली	दिल	dil	rib
गुर्दा	किलयीह्	kilyeh	kidney
फेफड़े	रियतान	riatan	lungs
अँतड़ियाँ	मसरिन	masrin	intestine
मांसपेशीयाँ	अदलात	adhalat	muscles
नाखुन	इद-दा-फिर	id-dah-fir	nail
पैर की ऊँगली	असबा ग्रैल कदम	asbaa ael kadam	toe
जिगर	कैबिद	kaebid	liver
मसूढ़े	लिस-सा	lis-sa	gums
खून	दाम	dam	blood
पेशाब	बोल	bol	urine
दायां हाथ	यामिन	yamin	the right hand
बायां हाथ	यासार	yasar	the left hand
बीच वाली उंगली	वुस्ता	wosta	middle finger
अनामिका	बिनसीर	binser	ring finger

Transportation
परिवहन

बैलगाड़ी	अरब।	araba	cart
घोड़ा	हिसान	hisan	horse

ऊंट	जमाल	jamal	camel
गधा	हिमार	himar	donkey
रेलगाड़ी	क़ितार	qitar	train
नाव	क़ारिब	qarib	boat
समुद्री जहाज	मरकब	markab	ship
साईकिल	बिसिकलेत	bisikalet	bicycle
ट्रक	सय्यारात शहान कबिरा	sayyarat shahn kabira	truck
हवाइ जहाज	तय्यारा	tayyaarah	aeroplane
टैक्सी	सय्यारात उजरा	sayyarat ojra	taxi
कार	सयारा	sayara	car
मोटर साईकिल	मातोसिकि	motosiki	motor cycle
ट्राम	तराम	traam	tram-car
हेलीकोप्टर	हिलिकोबतार	hilikobtar	helicopter

Diseases
बीमारियाँ

सर दर्द	वजा रास	waja ras	headache
पेट दर्द	वजाऊ बतन	wajau batn	stomach ache
दांत दर्द	वागा इसनान	wahgah isnan	tooth ache
कान दर्द	वजा श्रोतहान	waja othon	ear ache
टाइफाइड	तीफ़ूयीद	teefooyeed	typhoid
कब्ज़	इम-सक	im sak	constipation
कैंसर	सरतान	sartan	cancer

दर्द	अलम	alam	pain
खांसी	कुहा	kuhha	cough
जुकाम	जुकाम	zokam	cold
उल्टी	तकाउ	takayo	vomiting
खून बहना	ना-जीफ	na-zeef	bleeding
हैजा	कुलीरा	kuleeraa	cholera
गठिया	असबी	asbee	rheumatism
हड्डी का टुटना	कसर	kasr	fracture
अलसर	कुरहा	qorha	ulcer
दिल का दर्द	वजा क़ल्ब	waja qalb	heartache
लकवा	फ़ालिज	falej	paralysis
पेचिस	दिसीनतारया	disintarya	dysentery
खसरा	हास-बा	hahs-ba	measles
मिरगी	नौबा	nouba	fit
घाव	जुर्ह	jorh	wound
मतली	के-अ	qay-a	nausea
बेहोशी	इग्मा	ighma	swoon
फोड़ा	दुम्मल	dummal	boil
दस्त	इस-हाल	is-hal	diarrohea
चेचक	जुदरी	judaree	smallpox
इन्फ्लुएंजा	इनफिलवानजा	enfilwanzaa	influenza
तपेदिक	सिल	sill	tuberculosis
निमोनिया	इलती हाबिल	eltee habil	pneumonia
	हाल	hal	

प्लेग	ताऊन	taoon	plague
एलर्जी	हासा-सीया	hasa-seeya	allergy
सिर का चक्कर	दौखा	daukha	dizziness
सूजन	इस्तिसक़ा	estisqaa	dropsy
मोतियाबिन्द	सुक़ुत मा फिलऐन	soqut ma filain	cataract
अपच	श्रोसरी हुदमि	osri hudmi	indigestion
जलना	हुर्क़	horq	burn
कोढ़	बरस	barass	leprosy
खून की कमी	फ़ग्र दम्म	fagr damm	anaemia
ऐठन	तशन्नुज	tashannuj	convulsion
बुखार	हुम्मा	humma	fever
शरीर का छिलना	मरद-हुद	mard-houd	bruise
खुजली	जरब	jarab	scabies

Letter Writing
पत्र लेखन

1. Letter for Books
पुस्तकों के लिए पत्र

२४ भगत सिंह रोड
आदर्श नगर
दिल्ली
२६-२-१९८०

सेवा में,

व्यवस्थापक
पीकाक पब्लीकेशनस
नई दिल्ली

महाशय,

कृपया निम्नलिखित पुस्तकें ऊपर लिखे पते पर वी० पी० पी० द्वारा शीघ्र भिजवा दें, आपकी अति कृपा होगी :

१. ग़बन —प्रेमचन्द
२. कामायनी—जयशं   साद

आपका
रमन पाल

24 Bhagat Singh Road
Adarsh Nagar
Delhi
26-2-80

TO

The Manager
Peacock Publications,
New Delhi

Dear sir,

Kindly send the under-mentioned books to me on the above address by V P.P as early as possible. I shall be grateful to you for this :

1. Gabban—Prem Chand
2. Kamayani—Jayashanker Prasad

Yours faithfully
Raman Pal

Arabic

24 शारिया भगत सिंह
ब्रादर्शं नगर,
दिल्ली
26-2-1980

मुदीर दार उन नश्र प्रतताउम
दिल्ली ब्रल जदीदा

ह्य्यदी

तह्रीयनन व सन्नामन व बादु इन्नि ब्रर्जुकुम ब्रन तुरिसन जिन–

बरीद अलमजकूर फ़ीमा यलि मिन अलकुतब इला उनवानी । वं ऊना सब्रकून मश्कूरन लिहाज़ल मारूफ़ :

    1. ग़बन—प्रेम चन्द
    2. कामयानी—जयशंकर प्रसाद

अल मुख़लिस
रमन पाल

24 Shariya Bhagat Singh
Adarsh Nagar,
Delhi
26-2-1980

Mudir aar un nashr attaous,

    Delhi Al jadeedah

Saydi,

      Taheeyatan wa salaman wa badu inni arjukum an tursil bilbareed almazkoor feema yali min alkutab ila unwani. Wa una saakoon mashkooron lihazal maruf.

    1. Ghaban—Prem Chand
    2. Kamayani—Jayashankar Prasad

Al mukhlis
Raman Pal

+   +   +   +

II. Letter To a Friend
मित्र को पत्र

21 भगत सिंह रोड
नई दिल्ली
26-2-1980

प्रिय अशोक,

      तुम्हें यह जानकर बहुत खुशी होगी कि अगले मंगलवार मेरी मंगनी होने जा रही है । इस अवसर पर तुम्हारा यहाँ आना बहुत

अच्छा होगा । कृपया निश्चित दिन प्रातःकाल ही यहाँ पहुँच जाना ।

तुम्हारा मित्र
राजकुमार
21 Bhagat Singh Road,
New Delhi
26-2-1980

Dear Ashok,

You will be glad to know that next Tuesday I am going to be engaged. Your presence on this auspicious occasion will be very pleasing. Please reach here on the appointed day in the morning itself.

Yours friendly
Raj Kumar

Arabic

21 शारिया भगत सिंह,
दिल्ली अल जदीदा
26-2-1980

सदीकी अल अजीज अशोक,

तहीयतन व सलामन व बादु सतकून फ़रहानन बिमारिफ़ा अन खितबती फ़ी योमुल खमीस अल कादिम । व सोफ़ा नफसहू बि हूदूरिकुम फ़ी हाज़िहिल मुनासिबा अस्सईदा ।

व मिन फ़दलक उहदुर हुना सबाहन मिन योमुल खमीस ।

सदीकुक
राजकुमार

21 Shariya Bhagat Singh,
Adarsh Nagar,
Delhi Al jadeedah
26-2-1980

Sadeeki Al azeez Ashok,

Taheeyatan wa salaman wa badu satakoon farhanan bimarifa an khibate fee yaum il khamees al kadim. Wa sofa nafrahu bi huduri kum fee hazihil munasiba as saeeda.

Min fadlak uhcur huna sabahan min yaum il khamees.

Sadeekuk
Raj Kumar

+   +   +   +

III. Letter to father
पिता को पत्र

पूज्य पिता जी,

सादर प्रणाम

मैं यहाँ 25 तारीख को सकुशल पहुँच गया था । मेरे सारे सहपाठी और अध्यापकगण पच्चमढ़ी के दृश्य देख कर बहुत खुश हैं । हम लोगों के लिए हॉस्टल में रहने का अच्छा प्रबन्ध हो गया है । कल से हम अपना काम यहाँ शुरू करेंगे ।

बाकी सब समाचार ठीक है और आप किसी प्रकार की चिन्ता न करें । माता जी को मेरी ओर से प्रणाम कहें ।

आपका आज्ञाकारी पुत्र
रवि पाल

Respected father,

I reached here on 25th quite all right. All my class-mates and teachers were very happy to see sights in Pachmarhi. Good arrangement has been made for our stay in hotel. We will begin our work tomorrow.

Rest is all O.K. Please do not have any anxiety ove this. Kindly pay my respects to dear mother.

Yours obediently,
Ravi Pal

Arabic

अ्रबी अ्रलमुहतरम

इहतरामन व बादु इन्नि वसल्तू हुना सलामन फ़ी तारीख़ 25 व कुल्लु मिन जमालाई वल मुदरिसीन फ़रिहून बि मुशााहदतिल मनाज़िर फ़ी दिल्ली । व अ्रन्निज़ाम फ़ी सबीलि इकामतिना फ़ी फ़ुन्दूक तय्यत्र । व सा नव्दाऊ शुग़लना ग़दन ।

व कुल्लना विख़ैर व मिन फ़दलक ला कलिक फ़ी हाज़स सदद । व बल्लिग़ इहतरामी ्ला उम्मी ।

अ्रलमुख़लिस
रवि पाल

Abi al mohtaram,

ehtiraman wa badu inni wasaltu huna salaman fee uttareekh 25. Wa kullu min zamalai wal mudarriseen farihoon bi mush a hadatil manazir fee delhi. Wa annizam fee sabeeli ekamatina fee funduk tayyib. Wa sa nabdau shughalna ghadan.

Wa kullana bikhair wa min fadlak la kalik fee hazas sadad. Wa balligh ehtirame ila ummi.

Al mukhlis
Ravi Pal

×   ×   ×

IV. Sending Subscription to a newspaper
समाचारपत्र के लिए चन्दा

व्यवस्थापक,
नवभारत टाईम्स,
नई दिल्ली

महाशय,

मैं अपना वार्षिक चन्दा मनीआर्डर द्वारा आपको भेज रहा हूँ । कृपया मुझे अगले मास की पहली तारीख से नवभारत टाईम्स भिजवाने का प्रबन्ध करें । आप की अति कृपा होगी ।

धन्यवाद

आपका
सीमापाल
81 लारेंस रोड,
दिल्ली,

The Manager,
Navbharat Times,
New Delhi

Dear Sir,

I am sending you the yearly subscription for Navbharat Times by money order. Kindly start sending me your paper from the first of the next month. I shall be grateful for this.

Thanks.

Yours faithfully
Seemapal
81 Lawrence Road,
Delhi

मृदीरूत तहरीर
नवभारत टाइम्स
दिल्ली

तहीयतन व सलांमन व बादु इन्नी अब असु इलैकुम कीमतल इश–
तिराक अन तरीकि हवालातिल मालीया लि जरीदा नवभारत टाइम्स।
व मिन फंदलक उरसिलनी अल अरीदा मिन बिदायतिश शहरिल कादिम।
व अना सआकुन मशकूरन फ्री हाज़स सदद।

शुक्रन

अल मुखलिस
सीमापाल
81 शारिया लारेंस
दिल्ली

Muderut Tahrer,
Navbharat Times,
   Delhi

Taheeyatan wa salamam wa badu innee ab asu ilai-
kum keematal ish tirak an tareki hawalatii maleya li
jareda Navbharat Times. Wa min fadlak ursilnee al jareda
min bidayatish shaharil kadim. Wa ana saakoon mash-
kuran fee hazas sadad.

Shukarn

Al mukhlis
Seemapal
81 Lawrence Road
Delhi.

Vocabulary

चुस्त	नशीत	naseet	active
पता	इन्वान	enwann	address
पीछे	बाहद	bahd	after
बुरा	बताल	battal	bad
समान	अफ्श	afsh	baggage
स्नान का कमरा	हम्माम	hammam	bathroom
सवसे अच्छा	असहन	ashan	best
सावधानी	खतर	khatar	caution
सस्ता	रीखिस	rekhis	cheap
सिगरेट	सिगारा	Sigara	cigarette
मँहगा	ग़ालि	ghali	costly
खतरा	खतर	khatar	danger
माँगना	तलब	talab	demand
मुशिकल	साहप्रब	sahab	difficult
दरवाजा	बाब	bab	door
आसान	साहल	sahl	easy
खाली	फादि	fadi	empty
फ़ैक्ट्री	मसना	masnaa	factory
दूर	बाईद	baed	far
दोस्त	हबीब	habeeb	friend
फल	फ़ाखा	fakha	fruit
गैरेज	गाराजी	garage	garage
बाग	जीनीना	Jeneena	garden
अच्छा	तैयिब	taiyib	good

कठोर	साब	sab	hard
भारी	तॉकिल	tekil	heavy
हस्पताल	मुशतसफ्फा	mustashfa	hospital
भूखा	जाइऊ	jaaiu	hungry
बीमार	इज्ा	iza	ill
फ़ौरन	हलान	halan	immediately
ख़बर	खबर	khabar	information
अन्दर	गोवा	gowa	inside
बड़ा जेबी चाकू	मत्वा	matwa	jack knife
जिराफ़	ज़राफ़ा	zarafa	jiraffe
जंगल	गाबा	gaba	jungle
राजा	मालिक	malik	king
रसोई	मतबख	matbakh	kitchen
गली	हॉरा	harra	lane
बड़ा	कबीर	kabeer	large
शौचालय	कनिफ	kanif	lavatory
सामान	आह-अफ़श	ah-afsh	luggage
दिन का भोजन	ग़ादा	ghada	lunch
दवा	तिब्	tibb	medicine
पैसा	फ़ीलुस	felus	money
चाँद	क़मार	qamar	moon
तंग	दैयिक	daiyik	narrow
समीप	खुरायिब	khurayib	near
मांसाहारी	गाइर नाबाती	ghair nabaatee	non-vegetarian
दफ्तर	मकतब	maktab	office
केवल	बास्स	basas	only
जोड़ा	गोज़	goz	pair

पार्सल	रीस्सक	ressak	parcel
कीमत	थमन	thaman	price
शुद्ध	नसिफ	nasif	pure
कृत्रिम घाट	रसिफ़	rassif	quay
बरसात	मतत़ीर	matter	rain
भाव	सिर	sir	rate
कमरा	ग़ुरफ़ा	gurfah	room
हिफाजत	झामीन	aamen	safe
नौकरी	ख़िदमा	khidma	service
दुकान	दुक्कान	dukkaan	shop
थोड़ा-सा	बाद	bad	some
सूर्य	शम्मस	shamms	sun
नल	हनफ़िया	hanafia	tap
वहाँ	हिनक	hinak	there
प्यासा	झाह- झतशान	ah-atshan	thirsty
झन्दर के कपड़े	होदुम झल- ताह्तानीया	hodum al- tahtaneya	underclothes
बेरोजगार	बाततल	battal	unemployed
जब तक	लीगायीत	leghayet	until
ख़ाली	ख़ाली	kbalee	vacant
सब्जियाँ	कदरावात	kadrawat	vegetables
शाकाहारी	नबाती	nabatee	vegetarian
खिड़की	नफ़िदा	nafida	window
काम	शुग़ल	shughl	work
ग़लत	रूबुत	rubbut	wrong
क्रिसमस	ईद-झल-मिलाद	ed-al-milad	X-mas
युवा	जुरिग-यार	zoorigh-yar	young
जवानी	शवाब	shabab	youth